EXCEL VBA

PROGRAMMING

TABLE OF CONTENTS

Excel VBA

A Step-By-Step Tutorial For Beginners To Learn Excel VBA Programming From Scratch

Excel VBA

Intermediate Lessons in Excel VBA Programming for Professional Advancement

Excel VBA

A Step-By-Step Tutorial For Beginners To Learn Excel VBA Programming From Scratch

Introduction

Congratulations on purchasing *Excel VBA: A Step-By-Step Tutorial For Beginners To Learn Excel VBA Programming From Scratch*

and thank you for doing so. Despite the fact that most people don't know all that much about it, Excel is an extremely useful and versatile tool and taking this first step towards utilizing it to the fullest is sure to pay serious dividends in the future.

In order to ensure you have all the tools you need at your disposal, the following chapters will discuss everything you need to know about VBA, starting with the basics including accessing this feature in modern spreadsheets. Next, you will learn how to make the most of macros by using existing Excel data. You will then learn about the many ways both variables as well as If/Then statements can be used to take your macros to the next level.

From there, you will learn about some more complicated concepts include looping, as well as a number of additional tools that are sure to prove useful from time to time. You will then learn about common errors to watch out for while debugging and some additional tips for success to keep in mind while working with VBA to ensure you get started on the right foot.

There are plenty of books on this subject on the market, thanks again for choosing this one! Every effort was made to ensure it is full of as much useful information as possible, please enjoy!

Chapter 1

VBA Primer

While you can manipulate Excel to a fair degree through the use of formulas alone, there are always going to be tasks that require you to move and sort data in ways that are limited through the use of this knowledge alone. In these situations, it will generally be much more efficient time-wise to just create a program that can automate the task you are attempting. In Excel, these programs are known as Macros and Excel offers an easy means of creating your own through its own programming language known as Visual Basic for Applications or VBA for short.

The language operates via Visual Basic 6 which was a programming language in vouge before Microsoft standardized things with the .NET languages. While it was once quite popular, these days VBA is the last place most people will encounter it and even then in newer versions of Excel you have to manually activate the feature to even get a peek at it. If you pursue it, however, you will find that once you get used to it you will be able to easily create macros that will easily complete a wide variety of different functions.

While the language struggles with more complicated actions, as long as you don't push the limits of what's possible you will find that a little bit of studying will help to save a significant amount of time in the long-run. VBA can be found throughout the Microsoft Office suite of programs as well which means your new skill can have a wide variety of uses indeed.

First thing's first

If you are using a version of Excel from 2010 or later, you will need to enable VBA functionality before you can get started. This is due to the fact that some macros could, hypothetically, lead to security issues so Microsoft puts the responsibility of enabling it on the user. Luckily, the process to do so isn't difficult, all you need to do is go to FILE, then OPTIONS and choose the option for CUSTOMIZE RIBBON. From the resulting screen, you will then want to find the box marked DEVELOPER as doing so will provide a space for developer icons to appear on the main screen.

This won't do you any good on its own, however, as you have to use a separate option to allow Macros to be run within Excel. Specifically, you will want to select FILE, then OPTIONS, then TRUST CENTER and finally TRUST CENTER SETTINGS. From the resulting screen, you will then want to choose the option for MACROS SETTINGS. Finally, you will want to check the box marked ENABLE ALL MACROS.

Assuming you have followed these steps correctly you should now see the space for developer tools on the main screen and also run a program. If you can't do both successfully then you will know that you need to repeat the steps above.

Write your first program

If you have ever programmed something before then you likely know what is coming next. This is due to the fact that programming tradition demands that the first program you write is one that causes the message "Hello world" to appear on the screen. While this isn't the most useful program to run multiple times, creating it will help to get you used to the basics of VBA while at the same time ensuring you don't get into anything too complex which can make it difficult to determine where any errors might have come from.

In order to write your first VBA program, however, you will need to operate in something outside of the standard worksheet interface. You will be working in what's commonly referred to as a module which is a special type of workbook page. To get started you will want to locate the VBA icon in the newly visible developer tab.

To start creating your program you are going to want to use the command INSERT MACRO MODULE which will create an entirely blank page. Once you click on this option you will also find a new set of options near the arrows for REDO and UDNO. These new options include stop, play and pause and they will work just as you expect them to. Each module is also automatically named, starting with Module1. In order to change the name to something more descriptive, all you need to do is to locate the PROPERTIES box in the lower left corner of the screen and change the name you find there.

While working with modules, it is important to understand that they operate quite differently than your more run of the mill spreadsheet. The biggest differences you will notice right away is that the new page won't contain any cells and it also won't automatically calculate provided formulas. When you start typing what you will see are more traditional lines of text that you can then use the traditional paste, copy and cut functionality that you would expect from a Microsoft product. The module will save normally when you save the workbook as a whole.

One of the most important differences you will notice about the module is that it seems to complain about the text you type, regardless of whether or not what you are typing is grammatically correct. This is because the module isn't checking for spelling or grammar mistakes, it is checking for accurate VBA commands. This tool will be invaluable during the early days of your time with VBA when mistakes are likely to be far more common.

In order to ensure that you create a program that the module is sure to read, you will need to start the first line of every program in the same fashion by typing:

Sub *name* () with the name of your program replacing *name*. To create the program discussed above you will want to begin by typing Sub hell () which will serve to tell the module that the name of the program in question is hello. When you are finished creating a program you will want to ensure the final line of your program reads: End Sub. Without this line, Excel will assume that it is waiting for additional input.

You will be able to tell if you have entered a command correctly because it will automatically turn blue. This process will also include proper capitalization if you did not provide it as well. This will occur with any VBA keyword, which is a fixed set of commands that the VBA is programmed to automatically recognize. Luckily, the VBA is also programmed to recognize and correct common errors, such as failing to include the bracket in Sub hell () or forgetting to end the program with End Sub. It is important to be aware that this is the case as otherwise, you may end up creating even more errors by accidentally fixing errors twice. As you get more used to the language and what can be added via a module you are sure to find that it speeds things up a great deal.

Once you have the name, as well as the end and start point of the program, all that you are left with now is filling in the remaining middle bits. When working on a VBA program it is useful to think about what you are doing in terms of creating a list of instructions for the program to follow. As such, if your goal is to create a greeting at the top of the page then you need to give it an instruction to create a message box as well as what to fill it with. The easiest way to create a message box is via the MsgBox command. This command signals the module that you want to create a message box meanwhile following the MsgBox command with text in quotation marks like so MsgBox "message" will display the message in question in the message box.

With all of the pieces now in play, the process of display a message box that says hello becomes relatively straightforward. The program would look like so:

Sub hell ()

MsgBox "Hello World"

End Sub

In order to double check that the program is going to run successfully, all you will need to do is to click on the play button on the toolbar. If this part of the toolbar isn't immediately visible, you will need to check that it has been turned on. You can find the relevant option by selecting VIEW, then TOOLBARS, then VBA. You can also get the program going by using the command RUN, Start.

Assuming everything works as it should, you should now see a dialog box appear that will show you all of the programs you can run from within the current module. All you need to do is select the hello program and then select the RUN option. Assuming everything is working properly this will now cause the Hello World message to be displayed. You can then click on OK to dismiss the message and also end the program. However, if you had instead entered additional details after the first message, hitting OK would have brought up the next part of the message instead. However, if despite your best efforts, no message is displayed, then you will want to go back and retry the steps outlined above as well as check your code to ensure it doesn't contain any extra spaces.

Additional input

Once the starter program is up and running, the next thing you will want to do is to create a means for the user to interact with the program so they can add information as needed. To do so, you will need to use the VBA command InputBox which is similar to a message box just more complex.

The command for the InputBox is A = InputBox ("message). This will cause the input box to ask a question ("message") and also allow the user to generate their own response. The answer to the question needs to be numerical, however, something like "what is the number of pets you have". Any answer is then going to be confirmed via the Enter key.

Based on the above command, the number given as the answer would then be saved as variable A, if it was written a B = InputBox then the variable would be saved as B.

Variables are an extremely important part of most macros and you can think of each as operating in much the way that a named cell operates. The biggest difference here, however, is the fact that the VBA variable isn't tied to one worksheet as it will work throughout the full workbook.

When creating a VBA variable, the module will automatically track and store any details without you having to issue any additional commands. You can name a variable anything you like, though letters are used most commonly in situations where a full name is impractical. Once you have stored a value, you can then return to it again from any module in the workbook and it will be recognized.

As an example, if you were interested in finding out how many pets the user owns you would write the program as:

Sub hello()

    Pets = InputBox("How many pets do you have")

    MsgBox Pets

End Sub

When run, this will generate a message asking the user to indicate the number of pets they have before saving the results under the variable labeled "pets". While this might seem pretty basics on the surface, the truth of the matter is that it requires several things to happen at the same time. For starters, the MSgBox isn't displaying the word Pets and is instead displaying the number that was saved as the pets variable. This distinction is similar to adding a number to the A1 cell and then referring to it after the fact.

Taking things up a notch

While being able to generate simple avenues for output and input is certainly enough to allow you to create a wide variety of macros, it is still really just scratching the surface when it comes to everything VBA can do. The real fun will begin in the way it interacts with Excel directly, which you will learn more about in future chapters. Nevertheless, there is still more you can do with what you have already learned.

One prime example of this is a solution to the problem that arises when it comes to generating numerous sheets at once and making sure everyone using then understand what types of data need to go where. This is where a particularly useful feature of VBA, creating prompts, comes into play as it will generate a prompt at each place when someone needs to enter specific data.

With the following example, you will notice that the code has been simplified by ignoring the component that would involve the spreadsheet.

```
Sub loan()

    MsgBox "This program works

        out the total cost of the interest on a home loan."

        Amount = InputBox("The amount you will be borrowing from the bank ")

        Interest = InputBox("What is the amount you will pay in interest each month")

        Months = InputBox("What is the length of the loan")

    pay = Application.Pmt (Interest, Months, -Amount)

    MsgBox "Your total interest will be " & pay

    End Sub
```

While these lines are written normally for the sake of legibility, while typing them into the module you may very well find yourself at the end of a specific line without finishing a specific command. If this happens you will then need to continue the command on the following line to ensure it is read properly by the module when the time comes.

If you have set everything up properly to this point then when you run the above program you should see a message box that shows the goal of the program along with a series of boxes for inputs as well as the rest of the important information. You should also receive an answer once all the boxes have been filled in. You should not, however, just copy and paste the above code for use in a real-world scenario as it is missing check that makes sure users put in realistic values.

The important new feature in this example is the PMT function that is used to accurately figure out the full amount of the loan. This function also needs to be written as follows: Application.pmt (. This allows the VBA to understand that the listed function is generated via a spreadsheet as opposed to a command that came from within the VBA.

While this is a simple example, it serves to show an example of what a VBA macro can accomplish. What's more, it will make it possible for you to more likely accurately determine what is going to happen as well as what will cause it.

Chapter 2

Making Use of Data from Excel

Once you start working in VBA successfully, you will find that it becomes far easier to understand all of the possibilities of doing so. The trouble can being, however, if you find that you are having a hard time accessing information found elsewhere in the workbook. This works in stark contrast to a majority of traditional workbook functions where finding specific data is an extremely easy task.

Typically this process can be completed by typing something simple like =B4+B5 into a given cell and letting the worksheet sort out the rest. If you try this same approach in the module, however, you will find that the way this process works in the VBA is a remnant of its roots as a programming language. Thus, while its commands aren't quite as simple, they can be used in a wider variety of scenarios.

Locating data within a given cell

The easiest way to determine how these processes work is to start by referring to data that is stored in specific cells in a way that the VBA will understand. It is important to keep in mind, however, that there are going to be easier ways of reaching this data in the end, which makes this portion more of a thought exercise. In the following example, it is assumed that you were interested in accessing whatever is in Workbooks 2, cell G2 of Sheet 17.

temp= Application.Workbooks("Book2"). _

Worksheets("Sheet17"). _

Range("G2").Value

While this can be a lot of work to access the data in a single cell, it serves to illustrate how the code works as a type of address, starting with the most general information and getting more specific as it progresses. You will see this same type of pattern repeated numerous times as you work with VBA. It is also important to keep in mind the fact that various parts of the address are separated by a period while at the same time being read left to right as you might expect. To read the above address you would look at the application, which is Excel in this case, before finding the active workbook number, which is crucial when telling the program what to limit its search too. Finally, each workbook can then have any number of worksheets as well as cells within those sheets so the remaining information is honed in on even more easily.

You will also need to take note of the underscores that are placed at the end of certain lines of the code. These are simply used as a means of ensuring that the module reads the two lines of code as one complete thought. If you need to split a command between two lines splitting them with an underscore and a space is recommended. Underscores are what is known as a continuation character which means they indicate if a given instruction is spread across more than one line. While the module will most likely read the code properly regardless, it is often easier to insert these line breaks yourself to ensure everything remains nice and clear.

There are also a variety of different properties for cells that can be utilized, including color, height, width and more which is why Value is necessary in order to guarantee you end up with the correct value when everything is said and done. While all of this will certainly be useful as the groundwork for additional information, later on, it is only going to be needed in its entirety in very rare occasions.

Objects and properties

While this approach to finding the data in a specific cell can feel cumbersome to start, it is actually inline with a variety of modern programming languages so it certainly bears learning, even if you won't be using it all that frequently at the moment. The basic idea is that when working in VBA you will be working with Objects and these objects all have Properties. For example, if a specific cell in a spreadsheet is an object, and the properties within that cell are its values which means that the range B2 applies specifically to a cell that is also an object named B2 as well as the range ("B2"). Value can then be used to tell you if the value has a specific property.

While this is fairly straightforward to start, it can quickly become more and more complicated based on the fact that objects can also have other objects as properties as well. For example, if you are looking for an Application as an object then it can include a variety of different workbooks which are also objects in their own right while still being part of the Application's associated properties. Each of these workbooks could then contain a variety of worksheets which are then objects in their own right even though they contain cells which are objects as well.

This nestled functionality goes by the name object hierarchy and it goes application, workbook, worksheet, cell range. Each cell could also have additional objects associated to its properties though it is rare you will need to get that granular with anything. While this system might seem cumbersome at first, it is important to persevere as once you get a better feel for the arrangement of most objects your speed is bound to increase. VBA also features an object viewer that will allow you to easily view the hierarchies that exist within your module while also choosing objects from the list if you prefer. This will, as an example, make it possible for you to press F2 to look at the range for a given worksheet.

Simplify: After you are familiar with the general principles at play within the object hierarchy, you can then simplify things, even more, starting with the process for finding specific detail more quickly. To begin you will want to write your references with a specific set of properties so that you don't need to write out full names as you can count on several factors to be included automatically. These default phrases will naturally relate to the object of the required type that is currently active.

As an example, if you were to start out: temp = Worksheets("Sheet4").

> Range("B4").Value

This would tell the module that Excel is the application that is currently active and it would remember that fact moving forward. The same can be said if you use the VBA in other Office products like Word. The same level of assumption can be applied to workbooks that are currently active, assuming it is part of the same module. You can also let the worksheet autofill but this can be tricky in certain instances as it can become difficult to determine which sheet is currently active in a given model.

If you want to remove the need for a given worksheet reference you can write it as such: = Range("B1").Value. You will then want to ensure you runt eh code at least once to watch everything work properly. As you do so, it is important to watch and make sure the correct sheet is picked up. This will require to use the Activate method. Beyond properties, a majority of objects have methods as well. A method is simply something an object is asked to do. For example: worksheets ("Sheet4").Activate. This would, in turn, give the fourth sheet the activate method which would set it to the active sheet. This will be the fourth sheet in the current workbook, however, so it is important to set the workbook accordingly as well.

When it comes to creating something entirely new, you would include it like so:

> ub newvalue()
>> Worksheets("Sheet2").Activate
>> temp = Range("C2").Value
>> MsgBox temp
> End Sub

This will then help to ensure that things work as expected and that you are leaving nothing to chance as a result. This will ensure you see the contents of the specific cell on the specific sheet no matter what the state of things happened to be prior to starting the module. A side effect of this is that if you happen to close the module you will find that the sheet you indicated is now the active sheet.

The same overall process can be used to generate the correct workbook and would look something like this:

```
Sub findvalue()

        Workbooks("Example1").Activate

        Worksheets("Sheet2").Activate

        temp = Range("C2").Value

        MsgBox temp

End Sub
```

This will, in turn, help to ensure that the workbook with the given name is active, before then activating its second worksheet and then circling in on the cell C2.

With

After you have worked to make sure the module is looking for the specified data in the right place, you will then be able to go ahead and leave out those references moving forward as you can count on the module to fill them in automatically. This will not be the case, however, if you go ahead and reference several different workbooks or worksheets in short order. Luckily, as taking the time to switch them all over on your own can be extremely time consuming, you can do it without having to write out entire names. This involves the use of the command With – End With.

The goal here is that you can successfully quote a long string of names that you will eventually be using at the very start with a list inside a block. Doing so would look something like this:

```
Sub findvalue()

        With Worksheets("Sheet3")

        temp = .Range("C3").Value

        End With

         MsgBox temp

    End Sub
```

After the "with" the reference

```
    .Range("C3").Value
```

is expanded to

```
Worksheets("Sheet3").Range("C3").Value
```

From there, any reference that is placed between the With and the End With commands will need to be proceeded by a "." they can then be expanded upon in much the same way. The "." works as a type of invitation for the WITH command to include the rest of the name. it is also important to keep in mind that the above example takes advantage of the workbook that is currently active. You can then further specify the object that you want to focus on by using the With-End With command. For example, you would be able to indicate that Workbook3 and Sheet3 are the defaults for future With-End With instructions like so:

```
    Sub getvalue()

        With Workbooks("Book3").Worksheets("Sheet3")

        temp = .Range("C3").Value

        End With

        MsgBox temp

    End Sub
```

This can then be used with any object that is going to be considered the default With object…End With statement.

Using it: With this option on the table, you should now have a general idea of the best way to get at any of the values that you may have already added to a specific worksheet which means you are now ready to begin thinking about the many ways in which VBA and Excel can successfully work together. In most scenarios where you are choosing whether to implement what happens with the VBA or if a spreadsheet can do the job more quickly, some things are always going to need to remain on the spreadsheet in order to truly be effective.

One such instance is with the starter program discussed in the first chapter. It utilized inputs as well as a message box in order to utilize data entered by the user who was asked to provide an answer. The process was then taken care of by the VBA program and the data didn't actually utilize a spreadsheet in a meaningful fashion. As such, it could have been created in much the same way using any other programming language. Often, however, you will find that you are working with specifics that deal with Excel far more directly.

Back to the starter program, it could have been altered in such a way that it utilized data that was originally stored in the spreadsheet and had its calculations done directly through the spreadsheet as well. To do this all you would have needed to do was to create a new workbook before opening up the module and then using the INSERT command, then MACRO and MODULE before using the following:

```
Sub loan()

        MsgBox "This program works out the interest paid on a loan."

        With Workbooks("Book3").Worksheets("Sheet3")

        .Range("C3") = InputBox( _

            "The amount you will be borrowing ")
```

```
.Range("C1") = InputBox( _

    "Monthly interest")

.Range("C2") = InputBox( _

    "How long is the loan for")

.Range("C4") = "=Pmt(C2, C1, -C3)"

.Activate

MsgBox "Monthly repayments " & .Range("C4")

End With

End Sub
```

As written, this program does much the same thing as the program found in Chapter 1, except that it now uses values that were input from the cells in the relevant sheet and book. It is also important to take note of the With command in this scenario; generally speaking, it will be used to indicate specific books and sheets to act as defaults for any future references, here, however, the .Activate line helps to ensure the proper sheet is currently active. Finally, the message box displays any relevant information.

You should also be aware of the .Range command as it is useful when it comes to placing a full formula into a specific cell. Doing so successfully requires a bit of work, however, as the formula will need to be written with quotation marks to help ensure the VBA doesn't work to solve prior to placing the details in the specific cell. With this done, you can then switch to the worksheet and you will see the formula in question in the appropriate cell, just as you initially entered it.

You can get the same effect by adding the formula you wish to use to the cell manually, prior to opening the module. This will then require that the module make a handful of assumptions about the things that are stored in the worksheet, but certainly no more than most programs. In most instances, the module will begin by building as much of the automation for the given spreadsheet as possible right from the start prior to writing the part of the program that will require its functionality to be extended to an even greater degree.

The greatest advantage of this course of action is doing things in this fashion is that once a program has been properly executed you can still access the formula or data from the spreadsheet as normal which means you are free to change variables on the fly before running the program again to see what's changed as a result. This is where much of the true power of the spreadsheet comes from and where it provides a significant advantage when compared to utilizing pure VBA functionality.

If the program outlined above were written in its final form then it would have included additional titles and formatting to the spreadsheet side of things to help present all of the available information as effectively as possible. It would almost certainly have pre-included the secondary formula as well which means the macro would have been able to simply pull the data and show the results. In fact, these are two of the more commonly used roles that VBA programs play when it comes to working with spreadsheets that have a more complicated agenda. This doesn't mean that guiding the user isn't an important function, however, and you can easily use the VBA to provide relevant values and also check to ensure they are added properly to the worksheet.

Utilizing Ranges

Range object: The range object is arguably the main object you'll be using to interact with ranges. When you record macros in VBA and select a range of cells, Excel uses the range object. So if you selected cell A1 while recording a macro, Excel would record the action like so:

    Range("A1").select

In this example, range is the object. The parameter (argument) we're providing to this object is a valid cell reference (A1 in this case) which is provided as a string (i.e. in double quotes.) And the method (action) we're performing is "select" to select the cell, or range of cells, that was provided as a parameter to the range object. So we're telling Excel to find the range A1 in the worksheet (in this case, in the activesheet) and select that cell.

If you selected a range of cells while recording a macro, say the cells in the A1 through C3, Excel would record the action like so:

```
Range("A1:C3").select
```

In addition to selecting a cell, or a range of cells, you can also select a range of non-continuous cells. For example, you can select cells A1, B4, and D8 like so:

```
Range("A1,B4,D8").select
```

In addition to passing ranges, you can also pass variables that contain valid range references like so:

```
Dim addy as string

Addy = "A1,B4,D8"

Range(addy).select
```

All of these examples have shown the range object taking one parameter (a range of cells). However, the range object can take up to two parameters. The previous example of selecting cells A1:C3 can be written like so:

```
Range("A1","C3").select
```

You may be wondering why you would want to do this over the previous example since it requires more typing. In this example, the first approach would make more sense. But this flexibility can be useful as you'll see later when I discuss the current region property.

It is important to note in all of these examples the select method has been consistently used. This is how you typically work in the Excel worksheet. You select the cell, or range of cells, you'd like to work with, and then you perform some action on that range (e.g. insert a value, insert a formula, etc.) Because this is how you work in Excel, people typically bring this line of thinking when they start working in VBA. However, it is not necessary to select ranges to work with them in VBA.

Because it is not necessary, selecting cells is actually discouraged when writing VBA code unless it's absolutely necessary (unnecessarily selecting cells will slow down your macros.) Let's look at the previous example, but instead of selecting those cells, let's give them the value of 5. A property we can use to assign values to a cell, or range of cells, is the value property. So if we wanted to assign a value of 5 to all of those cells, we could write the example like so:

Range("A1,B4,D8").value = 5

This will input the value of 5 into cells A1, B4, and D8 without doing any selecting. Since no selecting is done, this macro is faster than a macro that does do selecting since it has less instructions to execute.

Cell property: The cells property is similar to the range object in that it can be used to interact with cells in a worksheet. The cells property is not an object like the range object. It's actually a property of the worksheet object. One big difference between the cells property and the range object is that the cells property can only interact with one cell at a time. Another difference is how the cell reference is provided. The cells property has two arguments: One argument is required for the row, and another is required for the column. Selecting cell B3 in a range would be done like so:

cells(3,2).value = 5

In this example, the row parameter is provided first (3 in this case), and then the column parameter is provided a second (2 in this case.) Alternatively, the second argument in the cells property can use a

22

column letter that's provided as a string. Here's the previous example, rewritten using a column letter:

Cells(3,"B").value = 5

Used range property: The used range property is useful for determining the range of non-empty cells in a worksheet. Unlike many of the previous examples we've discussed, it is not a property of the range or activecell objects, but of a sheet object. So, you can see the usedrange property of the worksheet Sheet1 like so:

Msgbox Worksheets("Sheet1").UsedRange.Address

The used range of a particular worksheet is determined by the upper-leftmost non-empty cell to the lower-rightmost non-empty cell. So, if you ran the previous macro, and only two cells in that sheet had values (e.g. A1 and E5) the previous macro would return A1:E5 in a messagebox.

When you want to use the usedrange property though, you can also invoke it on the activesheet object like so:

Msgbox activesheet.usedrange.address

If you used the activesheet object, one thing to note is that Excel does not provide intellisense whereas it does for the worksheets object. This is because Excel does not know what type of sheet the activesheet will be referring to until runtime. This is because the activesheet does not need to refer to a worksheet. The activesheet can also refer to a chart sheet for example. If that were the case, the previous macro would fail whereas it would not with worksheets.

One last thing to note is that, even though the cells between a used range may be empty, they're still included as cells in the range. In the previous example, using only cells A1 and E5 with values in the used range, only two cells have values. However, if you ran this macro:

Msgbox activesheet.usedrange.count

You'd see that it says that 25 cells are included in the used range. So, if you run a macro that processed all of the cells in a used range, it would be processing a lot of empty cells. This may not be an issue for a small group of cells like in this example. But let's say you had a used range with tens or hundreds of thousands of cells to process, with many of the cells being empty. In that case, using the used range would be very inefficient and the macro would likely be slow. There are a few strategies you can use to make the range in the used range more precise.

Chapter 3

If/Then Statements and Variables

Variables

The goal of this chapter is to teach you the easiest ways to initialize, declare and display different variables in VBA. Declaring a variable is the way you indicate to a given system that it should pay special attention to a given variable. Initializing is the name given to the process that assigns a primary value to a specific variable.

Naming variables: You're given freedom on how to name your variables, but there are some restrictions:

1. The first character in a variable name must be alphabetic

2. You can use alphabetic, numeric, and certain punctuation characters in VBA code

3. Variable names can be no longer than 254 characters

4. Certain words are classified as keywords and are not capable of being used as variable names.

Although these are not restrictions, here are a few other things to note about naming variables:

You can't write two different variables in VBA that differ only by case. If you create a variable named hw, and then later create a variable named HW, these variables will have the same value. This is important to note because some other languages allow this (e.g. C#).

Function names in VBA are not reserved keywords. So you can use the "left" name for the left function as a variable in VBA. It's recommended that you don't do this. If you do, you'll have to use vba.left to access the left function.

While you don't need to name your variables anything in particular, it's good practice to try to name them something appropriate for their purpose in your code so that others, or even yourself, can understand why you created them if they read your code. For example, assume you want a variable to represent the number 24. You can call this variable "b", but b in no way indicates why it's representing the value 24. You could also call it "hoursInADay" which is much more descriptive. This tells you that you're creating this variable because you want to represent the hours in a day.

Variable data types: All variables in VBA have a data type. VBA is known as a dynamically typed language. This means that you can either declare your own datatype or have VBA do it for you. If you don't declare a datatype, VBA will declare the datatype as variant and will try to make its best guess as to what datatype to assign it if a more specific one is available. However, this is not recommended for a few reasons:

By explicitly assigning a datatype, you can put restrictions on the types of data a variable will store. If you don't do this, the value of the datatype can be one you did not expect which can lead to bugs in your code.

One of the datatypes that VBA may try to use is the variant data type. The variant datatype is one of the largest datatypes in terms of bytes used in VBA. The variant datatype is large because it has the ability to handle any type of data. However, large use of the variant datatype can lead to poor performance. It's generally recommended NOT to use the variant datatype unless it's explicitly needed. (e.g. in variant arrays)

VBA supports several datatypes including the following categories:

Boolean: The Boolean (1 byte) datatype is a datatype that can store one of two values: True or False

Numeric: VBA supports a number of numeric datatypes such as Integer (2 bytes), Long (4 bytes), Single (4 bytes), and Double (8 bytes). These numeric datatypes differ by the range of values they can store. In these datatypes, an integer has the smallest range whereas double has the largest range. It's generally recommended that you use the smallest filesize capable of handing the range of numbers you want to use (or one above it.)

String: The string (10 bytes + string length) datatype can store text. So you can use the string datatype to store values like "Hello world"

Object: The object datatype is capable of storing any object reference

Variant: The variant (varies) datatype is capable of supporting many different values types, like string, numeric, etc.

Declaring a variable and assigning a type: To declare your variables, start by writing the "Dim" statement. You can write this anywhere in your procedure, but I tend to write mine on the first line in the procedure. To declare a datatype, you simply use the dim statement and the variable name like so:

    Dim hw

Although this variable is declared, it has not been given an explicit datatype. To give it an explicit datatype, you use the "as" statement and then its datatype like so:

    Dim hw as string

You only need one dim statement per line for your variable declarations. All variable datatypes in VBA must be explicitly named. VBA does not support declaring multiple variables with one datatype like so:

Dim a, b, d as string

Although all of these variables are declared, only d is given the datatype of string. The a and b variables have a datatype of variant. So to properly declare all of these variables as string, you have to write the procedure like so:

Dim a as string, b as string

Dim c as string

Forcing variable declaration (option explicit): VBA allows you to use variables and assign them values without declaring them. However, this is considered poor practice as it can lead to bugs in your code. It's generally recommended to turn on option explicit to force you to declare all of your variables. You can do this in the visual basic editor by going to Tools, options, and checking "Require variable declaration". If you turn this on, whenever you create a new module, the words "option explicit" will appear at the very top. You will get an error if you try to use any variable that you have not explicitly declared.

Determining a variable's type: Sometimes, it's useful to know what the type of a variable is. This can be very useful for both debugging and for using it in conditional execution statements. To find the datatype of a variable, you use the typename function and the variable name like so:

Dim a as string

Typename(a)

This will return the type of the variable (in this case, string)

Command button: The first thing you need to understand is that this process uses a command button which means in order for it to work properly you will need to insert one in your worksheet. To start, you will need to go to the Developer Tab prior to clicking on the Insert option. Next, you will need to locate the ActiveX control options prior to clicking on the selection titled Command Button. You can then drag the resulting button anywhere on the worksheet that you like.

At this point, the button won't be connected to a specific macro which means that it won't actually do much of anything. To link it to a given macro you will need to activate Design Mode. From there, you will want to right-click on the command button and then chose the option to View Code. Assuming this has been done correctly, this command should then open the Visual Basic Editor directly to the secion of code regarding the button. Next, you will need to locate the line that starts with Private Sub CommandButton1-Click () EndSub. In that space, you will want to enter the following: Range ("A1") .Value = "Hello:

Now, when you open the VBE a second window should also open that provides you with a variety of additional sheet names. This window is called Project Explorer and it will make it easier for you to see what sheet you are adding code to. If Project Explorer isn't automatically visible, you can find it in the view option by selecting the option for Project Explorer.

After you have entered the code you can then close the VBE, though you will need to save manually before doing so. The next step is to clear Design Mode and then click on the command button. Assuming the code was entered correctly the word Hello should now appear in the A1 cell of the current worksheet. Assuming everything worked properly that means you are now ready to move on to using more complex variables.

Integer variables: In order to store a variety of numbers for use at a later point you can use this code:

```
Dim x As Integer

z = 8

Range("B2").Value = z
```

The code above would then place the number 8 into the B2 cell. More specifically, the primary line of the code indicates a precise variable called Z in addition to the number 8. With that done, it will then initialize the value of x which is 6 as well as determine the location of the resulting equation which was A1. This means you will be able to change the range, integer, or value as needed. At the same time, an even more complicated formula for the button to solve could be included as well as variables from numerous cells as opposed to just one. You can also then add further variables as the need arises.

String variables: String variables come in handy when you need to store text instead of integers. Using the following code, for example:

```
Dim book As String

dog = "Labradoodle"

Range("A1").Value = dog
```

Would then add the word dog to A1. Additionally, if you had already used the word dog in a cell it would then be changed to Labradoodle. When you use this code you are declaring the first line which includes the string variable. The second line then indicates the variable as well as the additional change. When creating string variables it is important to keep in mind that quotation marks around the word are important. The final line will then indicate the new location for the variable in question.

Adding another variable: Doubling up on variables is useful when you need something more accurate than a single integer as it can store additional numbers after the decimal point. An example of this type of code would be:

```
Dim x As Integer

x = 6=2

MsgBox "value is " & z
```

Using this code would cause Excel to generate a dialogue box which will display the selected value of 6. This is not the correct answer, of course, which is why you need the double variable type beyond the standard integer type. To further make sure you generate the correct answer in this scenario you would want to write the code as:

Dim x As Double

x = 6.2

MsgBox "value is " & z

This code will let Excel know that it needs to check for a decimal place in addition to the primary integer and return the proper answer of 6.2. If you are looking to go past the first decimal point then you will need to use a long variable to do so. It is important that you use variables that are always of the right length in order to help your code run as smoothly as possible.

Boolean variable: In order to indicate a variable that can either be true or false, you will want to use a Boolean variable. An example of this type of code looks like:

Dim continue As Boolean

continue = True

If continue = True Then MsgBox "Boolean variables are cool"

Assuming it is written correctly, this code will then create a dialog box that expresses the proven fact that Boolean variables are cool. The first like of this code declares a Boolean Variable which is then initialized with a true value and the only Boolean variable is then utilized to help display the message correctly assuming the variables is considered true.

Statement types

If/then statements: An if/then statement is especially useful if you want a given line of code to activate only when specific conditions are met. In order to ensure this happens successfully, you will want to start by creating a button before then connecting it to the following code.

```
Dim score As Integer, result As String

score = Range("B3").Value


If score >= 70 Then result = "pass"


Range("B3").Value = result
```

The end result here is that if the score ends up being 70 or above it will be automatically labeled as a pass. This means if the integer in the first cell is 80 then pressing the button will add the word pass to the next cell over. As written the cells that are less than 70 would remain blank, though you can add an additional result written as < 60 = fail to have the word fail be displayed by those that did not pass.

Else statements: While secondary results can be added using the method above, an even easier way of doing so is by using an else statement which looks like so:

```
Dim score As Integer, result As String

score = Range("A1").Value

If score >= 70 Then

    result = "pass"

Else

    result = "fail"
```

End If

Range("B1").Value = result

This will, in turn, make it possible to assign a value of pass to the appropriate cells in the range that are above the determined value and a value of fail to the rest. It is important to keep in mind that this will only really work if there is an additional line of code after the portion of the statement and also if the statement doesn't contain any additional Else sections. If this ends up being the case then you can successfully add code to the line directly beneath the then statement as well as omit the End If line. This will, however, require that you start on a new line after the Else and then and also make sure you place the End line in the new appropriate location.

Chapter 4

Looping

L ooping is an immensely useful programming technique that will make it possible for you to run through several ranges quickly while only requiring the addition of a small amount of extra code.

Single loop: The first type of loop, the single loop, can be sued to easily move through ranges of cells that are one-dimensional. An example of this can be connected to the command button with the following code:

```
Dim i As Integer


For j = 2 To 7

    Cells(j, 1).Value = 75

Next i
```

Assuming everything is written properly, pressing the button at this junction will place the integer (75) in J2 – J7. This occurs because the line of code between For and Next is then executed five additional times. The first time that J = 1, the VBA knows to place the integer 75 into the cell where the column and row meet one another. From there, you will need for the VBA to hit the second j in order to increase the amount by 1 and thus reset everything to the For statement. Next, when j = 2, the VBA then provides a value in the form of 75 into the cell that exists at the next point where the row and column intersect. This then continues for all of the various cells and rows between 2 and 7. While this is not expressly required, with this type of code you are going to need to be in the habit of indenting to keep things as legible as possible. Specifically, this will comes into play between the words For and Next as this should make things easier to read when it comes time to find errors.

Double loop: A double loop is, as the name implies, a loop that makes a movement through a full two-dimensional cell range. In order to use one, you can use the following code and attach it to your command button:

```
Dim j As Integer, k As Integer


For j = 2 To 7

    For k = 1 To 2

        Cells(j, k).Value = 75

    Next k

    Next j
```

Assuming everything has been done correctly you will then find that this fills rows 2 – 7 of the columns k and j with the number 75. This code can then tell the VBA that when j = 2 and k =1 then it needs to enter 75 wherever the two meet initially, from there, it increases by 1 before returning to For in the k statement. Next, when j = 2 and k =2 then VBA knows to place 75 where they intersect again. Based on the code, the VBA will then ignore j moving forward as it will only be running between 1 and 2. This is then repeated until the VBA has run through all of the j columns that meet the desired criteria.

Triple loop: A triple loop is much the same as a double loop with the exception that it works across numerous worksheets. In order to use one effectively, you can use the following code:

```
Dim d As Integer, j As Integer, k As Integer
```

```
For d = 2 To 4

    For j = 2 To 7

        For k = 2 To 3

            Worksheets(d).Cells(j, k).Value = 75

        Next k

    Next j

Next d
```

When comparing this to the double loop code, the biggest difference you should see comes in the form of the variety of worksheets being used thanks to (Worksheets(c)). It is important to place it before Cells in order to properly ensure the first sheet has a two-dimensional range when it comes to c = 1, c = 2 for the second sheet and c = 4 on the third.

Do while loop: The loops listed above are what are known as For Next loops, another type of loop is the Do While Loop which can be used to make a given action repeat indefinitely as long as the process as a whole remains true. You can try one yourself like so:

```
Dim i As Integer

J = 2


Do While j < 7

    Cells(j, 2).Value = 25

    j = j + 1

Loop
```

With the code inserted properly into the command button, you will find that the number 25 is placed in the cells of the given rows. This works by looking for a j that is less than 7, in any instance where this is the case then the VBA will know to place 25 in the cell instead. When working with VBA, the = symbol means "becomes" rather than "equals". This means that $j = j + 1$ is akin to the point where j becomes j + 1 or if the value of j is increased by 1. For example, if $j = 1$, j really becomes $1 + 1 = 2$. This means that integer 25 will be adding into the column as many times as possible until j equals 7.

Now for a more advanced example, assume that you entered the integers 27, 35, 56, 59, 85 and 84 into the first six cells of column A. Next, place the following code into your command button:

```
Dim i As Integer

j = 1


Do While Cells(j, 1).Value <> ""

    Cells(j, 2).Value = Cells(j, 1).Value + 10

    j = j + 1

Loop
```

When done properly this should generate date within the first six lines of the column in question using the number 94, 69, 95, 66, 45, 37. The reason that this is the case is that for the length of time that the j and 1 cells value is not empty (<> is short for not equal to(, then the VBA will enter the value into the cell at the point where the column and the various rows intersect. The number that is entered is then ultimately going to be greater than 10 above the value of the cell at the relative point on the column/row intersection. Furthermore, the VBA will then stop auto-filling when j equals 7 as this is where the future cells will begin to empty. This process can then be used to generate a loop that is used for generating an almost limitless number of rows for a specific worksheet.

Chapter 5

Additional Tools

Autofilters

Creating the Autofilter: Creating an autofilter is extremely simple. You'll either need to have a header row or create one before proceeding. The following example creates an autofilter in the modules parent workbook on the first sheet from columns A to H.

```
Sub CreateFilter()


    With ThisWorkbook.Sheets(1)

        .Range("A1:H1").AutoFilter

    End With


'or simply

        ThisWorkbook.Sheets(1).Range("A1:H1").AutoFilter


    End Sub
```

Filter the Autofilter: You can filter any column of data by anything contained in the column. If you filter it by a value that is not contained in the column, it will simply filter everything out and you'll be left with only the header. In the following example, you will see the table filtered by a known value. Assume it's the table that was created in the above example.

```
Sub FilterATable()


    With ThisWorkbook.Sheets(1).Range("A1")


        .AutoFilter Field:=1, Criteria1:="yes"

        .AutoFilter Field:=2, Criteria1:="blue", _

            Operator:=xlOr, Criteria2:="red"


    End With


    End Sub
```

Notice here that the column has been filtered "A" for "yes" by choosing Field:= 1 and Criteria1:= "yes". Similarly, in the next line, the column has been filtered "B" for "blue" and "red". As you see above, an "Operator" has to be used to filter a column for more than one item and each subsequent criteria has to be followed with a number; first criteria is "Criteria1", second is "Criteria2" and so on.

The "Operator" is simple stating "I want to filter items that are "red" OR "blue". The most important thing to take from this example is that the range object only needs to specify a single cell in the header.

Autofilter with Variables: Here's where we can do some interesting things by integrating dictionaries into our macro. The situation is that you need to do multiple filters and do calculations with each set of filters i.e. you need to do some sums for each item category for each month. If you have 30 item categories and two months you're already at 60 manual filters and if you need to do 4 sums per filter, you can do the math. Check out the example:

```
Sub DataToDash()


    Dim oRow As Long

    Dim i As Integer

    Dim oCell As Range

    Dim oWB As Workbook, xWB As Workbook

    Dim oDict, oItem, oKey, xDict, xKey, errChk


    Set oWB = Workbooks("Your Book")

    Set oDict = CreateObject("scripting.dictionary")

    Set xDict = CreateObject("scripting.dictionary")


    With oWB.Sheets("Your Sheet")

        oRow = .UsedRange.Rows.Count


        For Each oCell In .Range("A2:A" & oRow)

            oDict(oCell.Value) = 1
```

```
Next oCell


For Each oCell In .Range("B2:B" & oRow)

    xDict(oCell.Value) = 1

Next oCell


i = 1

For Each xKey In xDict

    .Range("A1").AutoFilter _

        Field:=2, _

        Criteria1:=xKey

    For Each oKey In oDict.keys

        .Range("A1").AutoFilter _

            Field:=1, _

            Criteria1:=oKey


        On Error GoTo next1

        errChk = Application.WorksheetFunction.Sum(.Range("D2:D" & oRow).SpecialCells(xlCellTypeVisible))

        On Error GoTo 0


        .Range("A" & oRow + i) = oKey
```

```vba
        .Range("B" & oRow + i) = xKey

        .Range("C" & oRow + i) = "Top 25"

        .Range("D" & oRow + i) =
Application.WorksheetFunction.Sum(.Range("D2:D" &
oRow).SpecialCells(xlCellTypeVisible))

        .Range("F" & oRow + i) =
Application.WorksheetFunction.Sum(.Range("F2:F" &
oRow).SpecialCells(xlCellTypeVisible))

        .Range("G" & oRow + i) =
Application.WorksheetFunction.Sum(.Range("G2:G" &
oRow).SpecialCells(xlCellTypeVisible))

        .Range("E" & oRow + i).FormulaR1C1 = "=RC[1]/RC[-1]"


        For Each oCell In .Range("H2:H" & oRow + i -
1).SpecialCells(xlCellTypeVisible)

            oCell = oCell.Offset(0, -4) / .Range("D" & oRow + i)

        Next oCell

        i = i + 1
next1:

        Next oKey

    Next xKey

  End With
```

The basic concept here is to create a "Top 25" (luckily all of the accounts in these reports are top 25 accounts so we don't worry about filtering out non-top 25 accounts) category in the "National Account Name" column that does multiple sums for each "Item cat 1" per "Year/Month". This issue, then, is that we don't know how many or what item categories we have and we don't know how many months the data spans.

The simplest way to find out what we're dealing with is to roll these columns into a dictionary and see what unique values we're left with. That's exactly what the first part of this macro does, it finds unique "Item cat 1" and "Year/Month" values. Once we have these, all we have to do is loop the "Item cat 1" values inside of the "Year/Month".

Manipulating tables can be extremely time consuming and there's no reason why you shouldn't automate calculations that you need to do on a regular basis. By utilizing the Range.Autofilter method it allows you to write code that does not have to take the whole dataset into consideration when attempting to do calculations.

Collections

Collections are not only easy to use but can be utilized in a wide variety of applications. When you discover collections and the power they have, it will change your approach to VBA drastically.

Declaring & Setting: Declare a collection simply:

> Dim aCollection As Collection

Setting a collection is just as simple:

> Set aCollection = New Collection

The neat thing about collections is you can dim & set at the same time:

> Dim aCollection as New Collection

Adding/Removing from a Collection: Adding to a collection is quite simple and it involves Items and Keys. To add an item with a key:

```
aCollection.Add aItem, aKey
```

Keys are not necessary and for most applications will not be used:

```
aCollection.Add aItem
```

It's important to note that you can add any variable type to a collection. this includes ranges, sheets, books, and files.

In the same way remove from:

```
aCollection.Remove aKey
```

```
aCollection.Remove(index number)
```

Remove everything:

```
aCollection = nothing
```

or

```
Set aCollection = New Collection
```

Looping Through a Collection

```
For Each Item in aCollection

    Debug.Print Item

Next Item
```

```
For i = 1 to aCollection.Count

    Debug.Print aCollection(i)

Next i
```

Find something and perform an action

```
Sub Find_Add_DoSomething()

    Dim Type_Match As Range

    Dim Match_Collection As New Collection

    Dim First_Address As String

    With Sheets("Your Sheet").Range("Your Range")

        Set Type_Match = .Find("Your Find", , , xlWhole)

        If Not Type_Match Is Nothing Then

            First_Address = Type_Match.Address

            Do

                Match_Collection.Add Type_Match

                Set Type_Match = .FindNext(Type_Match)

            Loop While Not Type_Match Is Nothing And
Type_Match.Address <> First_Address

        End If

    End With

    For Each Item In Match_Collection

    'Do something to each item

    'Ex. Rows(Item.Row).Hidden = True

    Next


End Sub
```

Dig through folder/subfolder/files

```
Dim fso, oFolder, oSubfolder, oFile, queue As Collection

   Set fso = CreateObject("Scripting.FileSystemObject")

   Set queue = New Collection

   queue.Add fso.GetFolder("C:\test")


   Do While queue.Count > 0

      Set oFolder = queue(1)

      queue.Remove 1
'....insert folder processing here....

      For Each oSubfolder In oFolder.SubFolders

      queue.Add oSubfolder

      Next oSubfolder


      For Each oFile In oFolder.Files
'....insert file processing here....

      Next oFile

   Loop


End Sub
```

Dictionaries

A dictionary, like a collection, is a powerful tool to have in your VBA toolbox. Dictionaries are similar to collections and although a dictionary is a bit more complicated to manipulate than a collection, dictionaries offer some unique properties that are advantageous over collections like .keys, .items, and unique keys.

Declaring and Setting: Because dictionaries are not in the standard VBA library, a connection has to be made to the library. This can be done in two ways: late binding, and early binding.

Late binding is the easiest way to create a dictionary. This can be done in two ways:

With CreateObject("scripting.dictionary")

   .Add Key, Item

End With

or

Set dictNew = CreatObject("scripting.dictionary")

dictNew(Key) = Item

In both examples, the item is added with a key into the dictionary.

To use early binding it is required that you activate "Microsoft Scripting runtime" in the Tools-References tab. After this, declaring and setting becomes standard.

Dim dictNew as Dictionary

Set dictNew = New Dictionary

or

Dim dictNew as New Dictionary

Adding/Removing: To add an item/key pair to the dictionary

Set dictNew = CreateObject("scripting.dictionary")

dictNew(KeyAsVariable) = ItemAsVariable

or

dictNew("KeyAsString") = "ItemAsString"

of course you can mix and match AsVariable/"AsString"

It is important to note that a key can only be entered once in a dictionary. If you add a key/item pair with a non-unique key, the original item will be written over.

To remove a key/item pair: Set dictNew = CreateObject("scripting.dictionary")

dictNew.Remove KeyAsVariable

or

dictNew.Remove "KeyAsString"

CompareMode property of the Dictionary: This can only be set when the Dictionary is empty but allows you to control how the Dictionary accepts keys.

Dim dictNew As Dictionary

Set dictNew = New Dictionary

' Compare new key with existing keys based on a binary match. Essentially, case sensitive

dictNew.CompareMode = vbBinaryCompare

```
dictNew("Donut").Add "Sprinkles"

dictNew("donut").Add "Chocolate Glaze"

dictNew("donuT").Add "Maple Walnut"

' Remove all keys

dictNew.RemoveAll

' Set the CompareMode to Text. Case inSensITiVe. Donut == DONUT
== donUt == dONUt

dictNew.CompareMode = vbTextCompare

dictNew("Donut").Add "Sprinkles"

' ERROR! Duplicate key

dictNew("donut").Add "Chocolate Glaze"

' ERROR! Duplicate key

dictNew("donuT").Add "Maple Walnut"
```

You can also test if an item Exists in a Dictionary, which you cannot do as easily in a Collection

```
If dictNew.Exists("Donuts") Then Call EatEmAll(dictNew)

Sub EatEmAll(ByRef someDict)

    someDict.RemoveAll

End Sub
```

To do the same with a Collection

```
Set existsInColl = someColl("Donuts")

        If existsInColl = Nothing Then
```

```vba
        Call BuyDonuts(someColl)

    End If


    Sub BuyDonuts(ByRef someColl)

        someColl.Add 12, "Donuts"

    End Sub
```

Examples: This first example splits a notes section into 25 character sections while retaining the index number for each split up string and then prints the newly formatted data onto the sheet. The index number is in column A, comments in column B.

```vba
Sub String_Split()

    Set dictNew = CreateObject("scripting.dictionary")

    For Each cell In Range("B1:B" & Range("B1").End(xlDown).Row)

        For i = 1 To Len(cell) Step 25

            dictNew(Mid(cell, i, 25)) = cell.Offset(0, -1)

        Next i

    Next cell

    Range(Cells(1, 3), Cells(dictNew.Count, 3)).Value =
Application.Transpose(dictNew.Items)

    Range(Cells(1, 4), Cells(dictNew.Count, 4)).Value =
Application.Transpose(dictNew.Keys)

    Set dictNew = Nothing

End Sub
```

This second example creates a dictionary with the values in column A excluding duplicate values because they are set as the keys. It then sums all the values in the adjacent column and prints the unique values along with their summed values.

```
Sub Take_The_Cake()

    Dim rngAdd As Range

    Dim intSum As Integer

    Dim strAddress As String

    Set dicNew = CreateObject("scripting.dictionary")

    For Each cell In Range("A1:A" & Range("A1").End(xlDown).Row)

        dicNew(cell.Value) = 1

    Next cell


    For Each Key In dicNew.Keys

        With Sheets(1).Columns("A")

            Set rngAdd = .Find(Key, , , xlWhole)

            If Not rngAdd Is Nothing Then

                strAddress = rngAdd.Address

                Do

                    intSum = intSum + rngAdd.Offset(0, 1)

                    Set rngAdd = .FindNext(rngAdd)

                Loop While Not rngAdd Is Nothing And rngAdd.Address <> strAddress
```

```
            dicNew(Key) = intSum

            intSum = 0

        End If

    End With

    Next Key


    Range(Cells(1, 3), Cells(dicNew.Count, 3)).Value =
Application.Transpose(dicNew.Keys)

    Range(Cells(1, 4), Cells(dicNew.Count, 4)).Value =
Application.Transpose(dicNew.Items)

    Set dicNew = Nothing

End Sub
```

Chapter 6

Errors to Watch out for While Debugging

You might find some problems with your VBA code, but how can you debug the error? There are cases that your VBA code may require you to debug. Error handling refers to a code that you write to handle some of these errors when your application is running. These errors can occur as a result of missing a file, invalid data, a missing database, and many other reasons.

If you have a feeling that an error may occur at a given point in your code, it is advised to write a specific code that can handle the error when it shoots up.

Other VBA errors one can apply a generic code to handle them. This the time when the VBA error handling statement is important. It will enable an application to handle any error that is not expected.

To understand how to debug VBA errors, one must first know the different types of errors that exist in VBA.

Errors in VBA

The three types of errors in VBA include:

1. Compilation errors

2. Runtime errors

3. Syntax errors

Error handling is used to debug runtime errors. Let's now discuss each of these errors so that it becomes clear to everyone what a runtime error is.

Syntax errors

In VBA programming, if you type a line and press return, VBA will determine the syntax and in case it is not correct it will show an error message. For instance, when a user types an if statement and forgets to include the Then keyword, VBA will show the following error message.

Other examples of syntax errors include:

• Missing a right parenthesis i.e. c = left ("ABCD", 1)

• Missing an equal after I i.e. For i 4 to 8

Syntax errors are associated with one line alone. It occurs when the syntax of one-line is wrong. However, if you don't want to see the syntax errors, you can still switch off the Syntax error dialog box by navigating to Tools>Options and check off "Auto Syntax Check". This means that the line with a syntax error will appear red but the dialog box won't show up.

Compilation errors

Compilation errors will happen in multiple lines. The syntax is correct on a single line but wrong when the entire code is examined. Some examples of compilation errors include:

• A For without Next

- Calling a Function that does not exist

- Calling a Function using the wrong parameters

- Assigning a Function similar name to a module

- An if statement that does not have an End If statement

- Undeclared variables appearing at the top of a module

The screenshot below demonstrates a compilation error when a For loop does not have a matching Next statement.

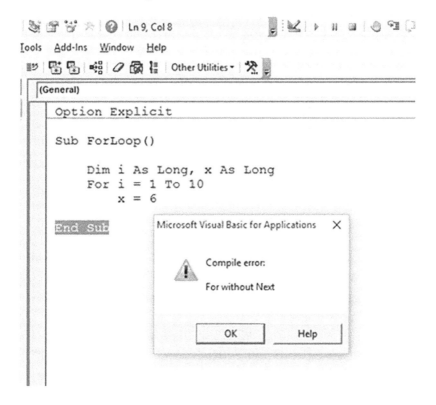

The Debug> Compile

If you want to identify compilation errors, the Debug > Compile VBA Project from the Visual Basic menu is important.

Once you select Debug>Compile, VBA will show the first error that it comes across. If the error is fixed, run the Compile again for VBA to determine the next error.

The Debug> Compile also has a syntax error in its search that is very important.

If there are no more errors left when the Debug> Compile runs, it might look like nothing has happened. But "Compile" will show up in the Debug menu. In this case, the application does not have compilation errors at the current time.

The Debug> Compile Usage

It is a good practice to always use the Debug>Compile before you can run your code. This will make sure that your code does not have compilation errors when you run it.

However, failing to run Debug>Compile means that VBA might come across compile errors when it runs. Don't confuse this with Runtime errors.

Runtime errors

As the name suggests, runtime errors happen when the application is running. These are the type of errors which you have no control. Runtime errors occur as a result of errors in your code.

For instance, assume that your application is going to read from an external workbook. If this file is deleted, VBA will shoot up an error when the code attempts to open it. Other examples of runtime errors include:

- A user typing invalid data

- A cell with a text instead of a number

- A missing database

Expected and Unexpected Errors

When you have a feeling that a runtime error may occur, it is important to write a code in place to handle it. For example, a code is always written to deal with a missing file. The code below first determines if the code is available before it opens it. If the file is missing, a message is displayed to the user before the code exits.

```
Sub OpenFile()

    Dim sFile As String
    sFile = "C:\docs\data.xlsx"

    ' Use Dir to check if file exists
    If Dir(sFile) = "" Then
        ' if file does not exist display message
        MsgBox "Could not find the file " & sFile
        Exit Sub
    End If

    ' Code will only reach here if file exists
    Workbooks.Open sFile

End Sub
```

Therefore, if you think that an error is likely to happen at some point, it is advised to add a code to deal with the situation. This kind of errors is referred to as expected errors. If there is no specific code that can deal with the error, it is considered an unexpected error. VBA error handling statements are important to use to deal with the errors.

The On Error Statement

So far you have learned the two ways you can treat runtime errors.

    1. Write specific code to handle expected errors

    2. Use VBA error handling statements to deal with unexpected errors

The VBA On Error statement is important to use to handle errors. This statement shoots a response when an error appears during runtime.

There are four different ways that one can use this statement

1. **The On Error Resume Next**. This code moves to the next line. There is no error message that appears.

2. **The On Error Goto-1.** This will clear the current error.

3. **The Error Goto 0-** This code will stop at the line with the error and display a message.

4. **The On Error Goto[label]-**This code moves to a particular line or label.

There is no error message that is displayed. This is mostly used for error handling.

Let's examine each of the above statements briefly

On Error Goto 0

This is the default response of VBA. Anyone who doesn't use On Error will see this response.

Once an error has happened, VBA will stop on the line that has the error and display the error message. Therefore, the application will need some user interaction with the code before it can resume. This may involve fixing the error or restarting the application. In this case, there is no error handling that happens.

Let's now look at an example:

In the code shown below, there is no On Error line applied. This means that VBA is going to use On Error Goto O response by default.

```
Sub UsingDefault()

    Dim x As Long, y As Long

    x = 6
    y = 6 / 0
    x = 7

End Sub
```

The second assignment line is a divide by zero error. If this code runs, an error message will show up on the screen as shown below:

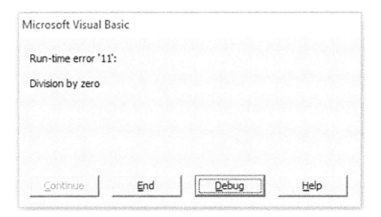

When this error shows up, you can either choose to end or debug. If you click End, the application terminates. On the other hand, if you click Debug, the application highlights the error line as shown below:

```
(General)

    Option Explicit

    Sub UsingDefault()

        Dim x As Long, y As Long

        x = 6
⇨       y = 6 / 0
        x = 7

    End Sub
```

This type of response is good when you are writing your VBA code because it highlights the exact line with an error. However, this is not suitable for applications that are created for users. They appear unprofessional and make an application unsuitable. This kind of error results in the application crashing. A user cannot continue without first restarting the application. In this case, users will not be able to use the application until the error is fixed.

But using the **On Error [label]** gives the user a more controlled error message. Furthermore, it prevents the application from stopping. This means that it is possible to force the application to behave in a given way.

The On Error Resume Next

The On Error Resume Next makes the VBA ignore the error and continue.

There are certain occasions when this is important. In most cases, you need to avoid using it. Adding Resume Next in the previous example causes VBA to ignore the divide by zero error.

```
Sub UsingResumeNext()

    On Error Resume Next

    Dim x As Long, y As Long

    x = 6
    y = 6 / 0
    x = 7

End Sub
```

Even though this makes VBA ignore the divide by zero, it is not advised to do this. If you choose to ignore the error, then the response may be unpredictable. The error is likely to affect the application in many different ways. Therefore, you could end up with the wrong data. Another thing is that you will not be aware that something has gone wrong because of suppressing the error.

The On Error Go to [label]

This is the correct way to handle errors in VBA. It is equivalent to Try and Catch function in C# and Java language. If an error happens, the error is sent to a specific label. This often appears at the bottom of the sub. Let's use this in the example:

```
Sub UsingGotoLine()

    On Error Goto eh

    Dim x As Long, y As Long

    x = 6
    y = 6 / 0
    x = 7

Done:
    Exit Sub
eh:
    MsgBox "The following error occurred: " & Err.Description
End Sub
```

Below is what happens when an error takes place.

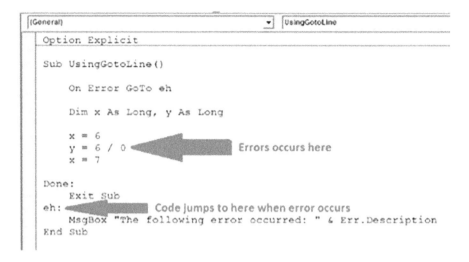

VBA shifts to eh because it has been specified in the On Error Goto line.

Note

1. The label that you apply in the On…Goto statement should be in the current Function. If it misses, a compilation error will occur.

2. If an error happens when the On Error Goto[label] is applied, the error handling picks up the default behavior. The code will remain on the line with the error and show the error message.

The On Error Goto-1

This is a different statement from the ones discussed previously. Usually, it clears the current error instead of setting a particular behavior.

When an error happens while using On Error Goto[label], the error handling routine returns to the default response. This means that when a different error happens, the code will appear on the current line.

This response only happens to the current sub. The moment the sub is exited; the error is automatically cleared.

Using On Error

So far you have learned that VBA will perform any of the following three things when an error happens.

1. Jump to a specific line

2. Ignore the error and continue

3. Stop and show the error

VBA will always assume any of the above situations. If you use On Error, VBA will change to the behavior that you specified and forget any previous action.

The Err Object

When an error takes place, you can review the details of the error using the Err object. If a runtime error happens, VBA will automatically fill the Err object with the details. To debug an error using Err. Study the screenshot below:

```
Sub UsingErr()

    On Error Goto eh

    Dim total As Long
    total = "aa"

Done:
    Exit Sub
eh:
    Debug.Print "Error number: " & Err.Number _
            & " " & Err.Description
End Sub
```

Err. Description: This contains the details of the error. This is the text that you will see when an error happens.

63

Err. Number: This is the ID number of the error. The time that you need this is when you are searching for a specific error.

Err. Source: The source will display the object name.

Get a Line number

The Erl function is perfect for displaying the number where the error happened. In the code below, Erl will return zero.

```
Sub UsingErr()

    On Error Goto eh

    Dim val As Long
    val = "aa"

Done:
    Exit Sub
eh:
    Debug.Print Erl
End Sub
```

There are no line numbers in this code, and that is why it displays zero. Many people aren't aware that with VBA, you can use line numbers.

The Err. Raise

This will allow one to create errors. You can use it to define custom errors for the application. It is similar to the Throw statement in Java and C#.

It has the following format:

```
Err.Raise [error number], [error source], [error description]
```

The Err. Clear

This is used to clear text and numbers from the Err. Object. In short, it clears the number and description. It is rare that you may need to use this in your VBA.

Simple Debugging Strategy in VBA

VBA has countless ways that you can debug an error. This means that it is easy to get confused about the type of error handling to apply in VBA. This section provides you with a simple error debugging strategy that you can apply in all your applications.

A basic implementation

1. Place the On Error Goto Label line at the beginning of the top sub

2. Place the Error Handling Label at the end of the top Sub

3. When an expected error happens, handle it and continue.

4. If the application cannot continue, use Err. Raise and jump to the error handling label

5. When an unexpected error happens, the code will jump to the error handling label.

The flowchart below shows how this happens:

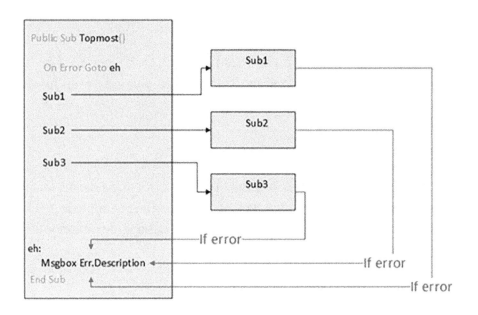

Chapter 7

Easy Mistakes To Avoid

When you program with VBA, it is easy to find yourself making mistakes. Most of these mistakes can cost you a lot. You will lose a lot of time as well as get frustrated. There are a lot of mistakes made in VBA code. If you go to forums such as CodeReview and StackOverflow, you will see many incidences of VBA code with mistakes. Usually, these mistakes are the same but committed with different people. Below are some of the common mistakes made by VBA programmers.

1. Use. select/. Activate

Did you know that it is not a must to apply? Select or. Activate? In fact, the reason why people use it is that they see it produced when you use the Macro Recorder. But, 99.9% it is not important to use it. Why? Here are two reasons why?

- It causes the workbook to repaint the screen. If you write Sheets ("Sheet1"). Activate, suppose Sheet1 is not the active worksheet, it means that Excel will have to make it so. This will result in Excel redrawing the screen to display Sheet1. This is inefficient and might result in a slower macro.

- It makes the user to get confused because they manipulate the workbook while they use it. Other users can think that they are getting hacked.

The only moment and occasion when you may need to use. Select or. Activate is when you want to direct your user to a particular worksheet.

If not, delete any line of code that has these. It is doing more harm than good.

2. Failing to use Application. ScreenUpdating=False

When you make changes to a cell, Excel has to update/repaint the screen to display the changes. This can definitely slow down your macro than the way it is supposed to be. The next time you are creating a macro, try and add the following VBA lines:

```
Public Sub MakeCodeFaster()
    Application.ScreenUpdating = False

    ' do some stuff

    ' Always remember to reset this setting back!
    Application.ScreenUpdating = True
End Sub
```

3. Failing to Qualify a Range Reference

One of the most popular bugs that people find that can be very painful to debug happens when the VBA code does not fully qualify the range reference. To understand what tot qualifying a range reference means, consider this code Range("A1"). What worksheet does it refer to?

Well, it points to the ActiveSheet. This is the worksheet that is currently seen by the user.

In most cases, this is harmless. But as time goes, you add more features into your VBA code and it takes a longer time to process. This means that when you run the code and click on a different worksheet, you will find unexpected behavior. This example may look contrived, but it demonstrates the point.

```
Public Sub FullyQualifyReferences()
    Dim fillRange As Range

    Set fillRange = Range("A1:B5")

    Dim cell As Range

    For Each cell In fillRange
        Range(cell.Address) = cell.Address
        Application.Wait (Now + TimeValue("0:00:01"))
        DoEvents
    Next cell
End Sub
```

If you use Range () and forget to highlight the worksheet, Excel will assume it is the active sheet. So, the way to avoid this is by fully qualifying the worksheet. You can change this part of the code:

Range (Cell. Address) = cell. Address to Data. Range (cell. Address) = cell. Address

4. Use the Variant Type

Another common VBA mistake is thinking that you are using one Type but the truth is that you have another one. If you look at the code below, would you say that a, b, and c belong to type Long?

Dim a, b, c, as Long

However, they aren't. In fact, a and b are of type Variant. This means that they can be of any type as well as a change from one type to another.

Any variable of type Variant is risky because it has been found to make it difficult to debug an application in VBA. It is important to avoid using Variant variables so that you don't make critical mistakes. There are certain functions which need Variant and you may not have any other option but to use them. However, if you can avoid using Variant types, it will save you time and cost to debug.

5. Reference a worksheet name using a String

It is normal to see people making a reference to a worksheet name in VBA by using a string. You can take a look at the following code:

```
Public Sub SheetReferenceExample()
    Dim ws As Worksheet

    Set ws = Sheets("Sheet1")
    Debug.Print ws.Name
End Sub
```

It looks like it has no issues, right?

Well, let's now assume that you submit your workbook to an accountant. The accountant decides to change the "Sheet1" to give it a more meaningful name such as "Report". Once the worksheet name is changed, the accountant attempts to run the macros using Sheets("Sheet1") and they find out that it doesn't work.

A simple way to fix this problem is to reference the sheet via the object directly, instead of doing it via Sheets collection. If you look in the VBE project window, you will see worksheets and correct names.

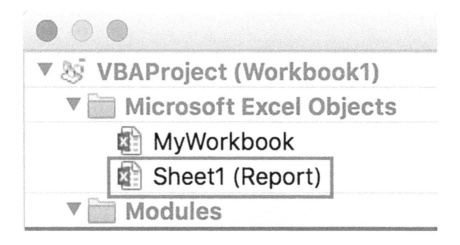

The name of the sheet that people see in Excel is "Report" and the name of the object that you can reference in VBA is Sheet1. Let's now update this code.

Now the sheet name is updated. What you can use is Sheet1 instead of Sheets("Sheet1").

But, what if one wants to make the name look meaningful? What if you want sheet1 to describe its action? Once Sheet1 was renamed to Report, it is a requirement to update the VBA code.

6. Make your Sub / Function Very Long

One rule of thumb is that if your function is very long such that one must scroll to see it, then you need to organize your VBA code. It is important to ensure that both the Sub and Function are short by creating sub procedures and helper functions.

7. Move Down the nested for / If Rabbit Hole

It is not a good practice to have a longer nesting. More than 3+ levels of nesting are considered long.

Whether you are a VBA guru who develops dashboards in Excel, or new to VBA, you only know how to write simple scripts that perform basic cell calculations, by learning the above mistakes increases the odds of writing a clean and bug-free code.

Conclusion

Thanks for making it through to the end of *Excel VBA: A Step-By-Step Tutorial For Beginners To Learn Excel VBA Programming From Scratch*, let's hope it was informative and able to provide you with all of the tools you need to achieve your goals, whatever it is that they may be. Just because you've finished this book doesn't mean there is nothing left to learn on the topic, and expanding your horizons is the only way to find the mastery you seek.

While much of what you have read in the proceeding chapters likely seems confusing now, never fear, with practice your skill with VBA will grow and you will find that you are able to automate a wide variety of useful tasks with ease. Don't forget, there is a reason that VBA is called a programming *language* as like any other language it is important to start slowly and take things one step at a time. As such, learning VBA is much like a marathon as opposed to a sprint which means slow and steady win the race every time.

Finally, if you found this book useful in anyway, a review on Amazon is always appreciated!

Excel VBA

Intermediate Lessons in Excel VBA Programming for Professional Advancement

Introduction

Thank you for purchasing the book, '*Excel VBA - Intermediate Lessons in Excel VBA Programming for Professional Advancement.*'

Excel VBA is an extremely helpful way to automate a routine task like copying data, creating your functions to reduce manual effort and increase productivity. When you use VBA, you can manipulate and customize data that is present in an Excel sheet. If you have read my previous book, you will have gathered some information on what VBA is. You would have learned about the different variables in VBA and data types, and how you can use them.

In this book, we will go one step further and focus on some important aspects of VBA. When you use VBA in Excel, you must also learn how to source data from one workbook to another without having to open the file. You also need to know more about working with loops and conditional statements. These statements make it easier to simplify iterative tasks. If you are eager to learn more about these aspects of VBA, you have come to the right place. Along with the points mentioned above, you will also learn about how you can manipulate strings and handle errors.

There are many examples given across the book that will help you understand the concepts better. Practice these examples before you begin to write your own code. You must remember that practice will make you a better programmer.

I hope you will find all the information you were looking for.

Chapter One

VBA, A Primer

Microsoft Office products like PowerPoint, Word, Outlook, FrontPage, Visio, Access, Project, Excel and some other third-party programs support VBA. If you have Microsoft Office on your device, you have VBA. VBA works similarly on all Microsoft products except for Access. The differences only relate to the specific objects of every application. For example, if you are using a spreadsheet object, you can only use it in Excel. VBA is currently based on VB 6.0, but there is a possibility that the future releases will migrate towards .net.

The focus of this book is how you can use VBA in Excel. VBA enhances the use of Excel by providing valuable features that you will not find with Excel formulas.

Macro Recorder

You can write macros in VBA in the same way that you would write a code in VB. The concepts of structures, variables, expressions, subprocedures, etc. are the same for both VB and VBA. The problem with VBA is that you will need to refer to every object you are writing a code for. For example, if you were writing a code for a specific cell in a worksheet, you would need to refer to that specific cell in your code. You are often unaware of what the names of these objects are and the attributes that you can control. The Macro Recorder solves this problem.

The macro recorder helps you develop a new macro in Excel quickly and easily. You must start the recorder and perform the necessary actions. The macro recorder will write the code for you. Alternatively, you can also run the VBA editor, which will allow you to insert a new module. This will give you a blank sheet on which you can write your macro. If you have already written the macro, you do not have to insert a new module. You will only need to add code to an existing module.

You will need to make some changes to the code written by the macro recorder. This is important to do when you need to change the cell references from absolute to relative or when you need the user form to interact with the user. If you have read the earlier version of the book, you will be familiar with VBA in Excel and some of the syntaxes and structures. Additionally, you must understand the differences between relative and absolute addressing.

VBA is different from VB in the sense that it is not a standalone language. VBA can only run through another product. For example, every VBA application you write in Excel can only run within Excel. This means that you will need to run Excel, then load the macro, after which the compiler will execute the macro. The VBA applications are all stored in the spreadsheet that they were written in. You can also store VBA applications in a way that will allow you to refer to them in other worksheets or workbooks.

When the application is loaded into Excel, you can invoke the application in many ways. Let us look at a few ways to run the macro:

1. You can assign a key to the macro when you record the macro. You can then invoke the macro by pressing Ctrl- "key." If the key is "a," your shortcut will be Ctrl+a. You must remember that the macro shortcut will override the default meaning of the Ctrl+a shortcut. You should also note that Ctrl/a and Ctrl/A are different.

2. You can either include an object or a button on the spreadsheet to call the macro. Go to the Forms window using the path Menu->View->Toolbars->Forms and select the command button. Now, draw the button on the spreadsheet. Choose the macro that

you want to link to the button when the dialog box or prompt opens. You can also include pictures and other objects and assign macros to them.

3. Select the macro from the menu and run it. Go to the Macros section using the following path Menu->Tools->Macro->Macros and choose the macro you want to run.

4. You can also use the VBA editor to run the macro. You can either click on the run button to run the macro or go through each line of the code while giving yourself time to debug the code. When you are debugging the code, you should move the VBA editor into a pane adjacent to the spreadsheet and execute the code to see what is happening.

If you choose to name a macro "Sub Auto_Open()," this macro will run when you load or open the spreadsheet. This will only happen if you have enabled macros.

Security and Macro Storage

For every Microsoft Office application, there are three security levels for macros. The macro security level is always set to high by default. To change the security of your macro, go to the security tab and make your selection. Go to Menu->Tools->Security Tab->Macro Security.

The three security levels for macros are:

1. High: The macros that are signed by a trusted source will run in Excel. If there is any unsigned macro, it will automatically be disabled.

2. Medium: This is the recommended setting since you can choose to enable or disable a macro.

3. Low: This is not recommended since the macros are loaded into the workbook without notifying the user.

If you know you will be using macros, you should set the security of the macros to medium. When you load the spreadsheet, Excel will ask you if you want to enable or disable a macro. If you know that a specific sheet contains a macro and you know who wrote it, you can enable it.

Since there are some macros that are set to run when you open a spreadsheet, it is not possible for you to always have the chance to examine the macro before you enable it. It is important to remember that an Excel Macro virus is very rare. This is because a macro is only available on the spreadsheet where it was written. Macros are always stored in the workbook by default and every time you load the workbook, the macros are loaded.

When you create a macro for the first time, you can decide where to store the macro. The best choices are:

1. This Workbook: The macro is stored in the worksheet where it is written. Anybody who has access to the worksheet can access the macro.

2. Personal Macro Workbook: All the macros on your PC are stored in this workbook. Only when you copy the macro and save it with the spreadsheet will others be able to view the macro.

You can use the VBA editor to see where the macros are stored. The Project Explorer Window, on the upper left of the screen, shows you where the files are placed and their hierarchy. You can use the Explorer to view, move, copy or delete a macro.

Chapter Two

How to Use Data from Excel

There will be times when you do not want to manually copy data from one Excel file to another. If you automate this procedure, you can ensure that the data is entered accurately, there is no duplication in the data and the figures will not be entered in an incorrect location. This will also save time.

You can write the code to perform this function in the Workbook_Open() event or function in ThisWorkBook object in VBA. When you write this code in the Workbook_Open() function, the compiler will ensure that the figures are updated correctly when the source Excel file is open.

To develop the code, open the destination excel file and press Alt+F8. You will find the ThisWorkbook module under the Microsoft Excel Objects in Project Explorer. Open the window and from the object dropdown list, choose "Workbook."

Option Explicit

> Private Sub Workbook_Open()
>
> > Call ReadDataFromCloseFile
>
> End Sub

```vba
Sub ReadDataFromCloseFile()

    On Error GoTo ErrHandler

    Application.ScreenUpdating = False

        Dim src As Workbook

        ' OPEN THE SOURCE EXCEL WORKBOOK IN "READ
ONLY MODE."

        Set src = Workbooks.Open("C:\Q-SALES.xlsx", True, True)

        ' GET THE TOTAL ROWS FROM THE SOURCE
WORKBOOK.

        Dim iTotalRows As Integer

        iTotalRows = src.Worksheets("sheet1").Range("B1:B" &
Cells(Rows.Count, "B").End(xlUp).Row).Rows.Count

        ' COPY DATA FROM SOURCE (CLOSE
WORKGROUP) TO THE DESTINATION WORKBOOK.

        Dim iCnt As Integer        ' COUNTER.

    For iCnt = 1 To iTotalRows

        Worksheets("Sheet1").Range("B" & iCnt).Formula =

            src.Worksheets("Sheet1").Range("B" & iCnt).Formula

    Next iCnt

        ' CLOSE THE SOURCE FILE.

        src.Close False            ' FALSE - DON'T SAVE THE
SOURCE FILE.

        Set src = Nothing
```

ErrHandler:

Application.EnableEvents = True

Application.ScreenUpdating = True

End Sub

Property Application.ScreenUpdating

In the first line of the code, you will see that the Application.ScreenUpdating property is set to false. This is done to increase the speed of the macro that you have written.

Open the Source File and Read Data

We are then opening the source workbook to read or copy the data from it. Excel will only open the file in the read only state. This means that it will make no changes to the source file.

Set src = Workbooks.Open("C:\Q-SALES.xlsx", True, True)

Once you have obtained the data, the compiler will count the number of rows present in the source workbook. The loop will run and the data will be copied from the source and pasted into the destination workbook.

' COPY DATA FROM SOURCE (CLOSE WORKGROUP) TO THE DESTINATION FILE.

For iCnt = 1 To iTotalRows

Worksheets("Sheet1").Range("B" & iCnt).Formula =

src.Worksheets("Sheet1").Range("B" & iCnt).Formula

Next iCnt

You should then close the source file and finally set the property Application.ScreenUpdating to true.

Chapter Three

Working With Loops

One of the most powerful and basic programming tools available in VBA is a loop. This tool is used across many programming languages where the programmer wants to repeat a block of code until a condition holds true or until a specific point. If the condition is false, the loop will break and the section of code after the loop is executed. By using loops, you can write a few lines of code and achieve significant output.

The For Loop

For…Next Statement

The For…Next Loop will repeat a statement or a block of code for a specific number of iterations. The syntax for the loop is as follows:

```
For counter_variable = start_value To end_value

[block of code]

Next counter_variable
```

Let us look at a simple example of how to use this loop.

```
Sub forNext1()

Dim i As Integer

Dim iTotal As Integer

iTotal = 0
```

For i = 1 To 5

iTotal = i + iTotal

Next i

MsgBox iTotal

End Sub

The For Each … Next Statement

If you want to repeat a block of code for every object or variable in a group, you should use the For Each…Next Loop. This statement will repeat the execution of a block of code or statements for every element in the collection. The loop will stop when every element in the collection is covered. The execution will immediately move to that section of code that is immediately after the Next statement. The syntax of the loop is as follows:

For Each object_variable In group_object_variable

[block of code]

Next object_variable

Example 1

In the example below, the loop will go through every worksheet in the workbook. VBA will execute the code which will protect the worksheets with a password. In this example, the variable ws is the Worksheet Object variable. The group or collection of worksheets is present in this workbook.

Sub forEach1()

Dim ws As Worksheet

For Each ws In ThisWorkbook.Worksheets

```
ws.Protect Password:="123"

Next ws

End Sub
```

Example 2

In the example below, the VBA will iterate through every cell in the range A1:A10. The code will set the background color of every cell to yellow. In this example, rCell is the Range Object variable, and the collection or group of cells is present in Range("A1:A10").

```
Sub forEach2()

Dim rCell As Range

For Each rCell In ActiveSheet.Range("A1:A10")

rCell.Interior.Color = RGB(255, 255, 0)

Next rCell

End Sub
```

Nesting Loops

If you want to include more than one condition in a loop, you can use nesting. You can create a nested loop by adding one loop to another. You can add an infinite number of loops if you are creating a nested loop. You can also nest one type of a loop inside another type of loop.

If you are using a For Loop, it is important that the inner loop is completed first. It is only after the inner loop is fully complete that the statements below the Next statement of the inner loop are executed. Alternatively, you can nest one type of control structure in another.

In the example below, we will use an IF statement in a WITH statement that is within a For…Each Loop. VBA will go through every cell in the range A1:A10. If the value of the cell exceeds 5, VBA will color the cell as Yellow. Otherwise, it will color the cells red.

```
Sub nestingLoops()

Dim rCell As Range

For Each rCell In ActiveSheet.Range("A1:A10")

With rCell

If rCell > 5 Then

.Interior.Color = RGB(255, 255, 0)

Else

.Interior.Color = RGB(255, 0, 0)

End If

End With

Next rCell

End Sub
```

The Exit For Statement

You can use the Exit For statement to exit the For Loop without completing the full cycle. This means that you will be exiting the For Loop early. This statement will instruct VBA to stop the execution of the loop and move to the section or block of code at the end of the loop, or the code that follows the Next statement. If you are using Nested loops, VBA will stop the execution of the code in the inner level and move to the outer level. You should use this statement wen you want to terminate the loop once it has satisfied a condition or reached a specific value. You can also use this statement to break an endless loop after a certain point.

Let us look at the following example:

In the example below, if the value of Range("A1") is blank, the value of the variable iTotal will be 55. If Range("A1") has the value 5, VBA will terminate the loop when the counter reaches the value 5. At this point, the value of iTotal will be 15. You should note that the loop will run until the counter value reaches 5, after which it will exit the loop.

```
Sub exitFor1()

Dim i As Integer

Dim iTotal As Integer

iTotal = 0

For i = 1 To 10

iTotal = i + iTotal

If i = ActiveSheet.Range("A1") Then

Exit For

End If

Next i

MsgBox iTotal

End Sub
```

The Do While Loop

You can use the Do While Loop to repeat a block of code or statements indefinitely as long as the condition is met and the value is True. VBA will stop executing the block of code when the condition returns the value False. You can test the condition either at the start or at the end of the loop. The Do While...Loop statement is where the condition is tested at the start while the Do...Loop While statement is the condition that is tested at the end of the loop. When the condition at the start of the loop is not met, the former loop will not execute the block of code in the loop. The latter statement will function at least once since the condition is at the end of the loop.

Do While…Loop Statement

The syntax for the loop is:

> Do While [Condition]
>
> [block of code]
>
> Loop

Do…Loop While Statement

The syntax for the loop is:

> Do
>
> [block of code]
>
> Loop While [Condition]

The loops are explained below with the help of examples.

Example 1

In the example below, the condition is tested at the beginning of the loop. Since the condition is not met, the loop will not execute, and the value of iTotal will be zero.

> Sub doWhile1()
>
> Dim i As Integer
>
> Dim iTotal As Integer
>
> i = 5

```
iTotal = 0

Do While i > 5

iTotal = i + iTotal

i = i - 1

Loop

MsgBox iTotal

End Sub
```

Example 2

In the example below, the condition is only tested at the end of the function. Since the condition is true, the loop will execute once. It will terminate after that since the value of I will reduce to 4, and the variable iTotal will return the value 5.

```
Sub doWhile2()

Dim i As Integer

Dim iTotal As Integer

i = 5

iTotal = 0

Do

iTotal = i + iTotal

i = i - 1

Loop While i > 5

MsgBox iTotal

End Sub
```

Example 3

In this example, we will replace the blanks in a range of cells with underscores.

```vba
Sub doWhile3()

Dim rCell As Range

Dim strText As String

Dim n As Integer

'rCell is a Cell in the specified Range which contains the strText

'strText is the text in a Cell in which blank spaces are to be replaced with underscores

'n is the position of blank space(s) occurring in a strText

For Each rCell In ActiveSheet.Range("A1:A5")

strText = rCell

'the VBA InStr function returns the position of the first occurrence of a string within another string. Using this to determine the position of the first blank space in the strText.

n = InStr(strText, " ")

Do While n > 0

'blank space is replaced with the underscore character in the strText

strText = Left(strText, n - 1) & "_" & Right(strText, Len(strText) - n)

'Use this line of code instead of the preceding line, to remove all blank spaces in the strText
```

```
'strText= Left(strText, n - 1) & Right(strText, Len(strText) - n)

n = InStr(strText, " ")

Loop

rCell = strText

Next



End Sub
```

The Exit Do Statement

You can use the Exit Do Statement to exit the Do While Loop before you complete the cycle. The Exit Do statement will instruct VBA to stop executing the lines of code in the loop and move to the block of code that is immediately after the loop. If it is a nested loop, the statement will instruct VBA to execute the lines of code in the outer loop. You can use an infinite number of Exit Do statements in a loop, and this statement is useful when you want to terminate the loop once you obtain the desired value. This is similar to the Exit For statement.

Let us look at the following example. In the example below, the iTotal will be 55 is Range("A1") is blank. If it contains the number 5, VBA will terminate the loop when the value of the counter is 5. The value of iTotal will increase to 10.

```
Sub exitDo1()

Dim i As Integer

Dim iTotal As Integer

iTotal = 0

Do While i < 11
```

iTotal = i + iTotal

i = i + 1

If i = ActiveSheet.Range("A1") Then

Exit Do

End If

Loop

MsgBox iTotal

End Sub

The Do Until Loop

When you use the Do Until Loop, VBA will repeat the block of code indefinitely until the specified condition is true. You can use this statement to test the condition either at the start or at the end of the loop. The Do Until…Loop statement will test the condition at the start of the loop while the Do…Loop Until statement will test the condition at the end of the loop. In the former statement, if the condition is false, VBA will not execute the block of code within the statement since the condition has to hold true right from the start. In the latter statement, the block of code in the loop will execute at least once since the condition is at the end of the loop.

Do Until…Loop Statement

The syntax for the statement is below:

Do Until [Condition]

[block of code]

Loop

Do...Loop Until Statement

The syntax for the statement is below:

Do

[block of code]

Loop Until [Condition]

Let us look at the following statements using the following examples.

Example 1

In this example, VBA will color every empty cell yellow until it encounters a non-empty cell. If there is a non-empty cell at the start, the code will not execute since the condition is mentioned at the beginning of the loop.

```
Sub doUntil1()

Dim rowNo As Integer

rowNo = 1

Do Until Not IsEmpty(Cells(rowNo, 1))

Cells(rowNo, 1).Interior.Color = RGB(255, 255, 0)

rowNo = rowNo + 1

Loop

End Sub
```

Example 2

In this example, VBA will color every empty cell yellow until it encounters a non-empty cell. If there is a non-empty cell at the start, the code will execute at least once since the condition is mentioned at the end of the loop.

```
Sub doUntil2()

Dim rowNo As Integer

rowNo = 1

Do

Cells(rowNo, 1).Interior.Color = RGB(255, 255, 0)

rowNo = rowNo + 1

Loop Until Not IsEmpty(Cells(rowNo, 1))

End Sub
```

The Exit Do Statement

You can use the Exit Do statement to exit the Do Until Loop without completing a full cycle. This is similar to the Do While Loop that we looked at earlier.

Chapter Four

Working With Conditional Statements

There are two conditional statements that you can use in VBA:

1. If…Then…Else

2. Select…Case

In both these conditional statements, VBA will need to evaluate one or more conditions after which the block of code between the parentheses is executed. These statements are executed depending on what the result of the evaluation is.

If…Then…Else Statements

This conditional statement will execute a block of statements or code when the condition is met.

Multiple-line Statements

> *If condition Then*
>
> *statements*
>
> *ElseIf elseif_condition_1 Then*
>
> *elseif_statements_1*
>
> *ElseIf elseif_condition_n Then*
>
> *elseif_statements_n*
>
> *Else*

else_statements

End If

Let us break the statements down to understand what each part of the block of code written above means.

If Statement

If you want to write a multiple-line syntax, like the example above, the first line of the code should only contain the 'If' statement. We will cover the single-line syntax in the following section.

Condition

This is an expression that could either be a string or numeric. The compiler will evaluate this condition and return either true or false. It is necessary to define a condition.

Statements

These statements make up the block of code that the compiler will execute if the condition is true. If you do not specify a statement, then the compiler will not execute any code even if the condition is true.

ElseIf

This is a clause that can be used if you want to include multiple conditions. If you have an ElseIf in the code, you need to specify the elseif_condition. You can include an infinite number of ElseIf and elseif_conditions in your code.

elseif_condition

This is an expression that the compiler will need to evaluate. The result of the expression should either be true or false.

Elseif_statements

These statements or blocks of code are evaluated if the compiler returns the result true for the elseif_condition. If you do not specify a statement, then the compiler will not execute any code even if the condition is true.

The Else -> condition and elseif_conditions are always tested in the order they are written in. If any condition is true, the block of code that comes immediately after the condition will be executed. If no conditions in the elseif_conditions returns the value the true, the block of code after the **Else** clause will be executed. You can choose to include the Else in the If…Then…Else statement.

else_statements

These statements are the blocks of code written immediately after the Else statement.

End If

This statement terminates the If…Then…Else block of statements and it is important that you mention these keywords at the end of the block.

Nesting

You can nest the If…Then…Else statements in a loop using the Select…Case or VBA Loops (covered in the previous chapter), without a limit. If you are using Excel 2003, you can only use 7 levels of nesting, but if you use Excel 2007, you can use 64. The latest versions of Excel allow a larger level of nesting.

Let us look at the following example:

Example 1

```
Sub ElseIfStructure()

'Returns Good if the marks are equal to 60.

Dim sngMarks As Single

sngMarks = 60

If sngMarks >= 80 Then

MsgBox "Excellent"

ElseIf sngMarks >= 60 And sngMarks < 80 Then

MsgBox "Good"

ElseIf sngMarks >= 40 And sngMarks < 60 Then

MsgBox "Average"

Else

MsgBox "Poor"

End If

End Sub
```

Example 2

In this example, we will use Multiple If…Then Statements. This is an alternative to the ElseIf structure, but is not as efficient as the ElseIf Structure. In the Multiple If…Then Statements, the compiler will need to run through every If…Then block of code even after it returns the result true for one of the conditions. If you use the ElseIf structure, the subsequent conditions are not checked if one condition is true. This makes the ElseIf structure faster. If you can perform the function using the ElseIf structure, you should avoid using the Multiple If…Then Structure.

```
Sub multipleIfThenStmnts()

"Returns Good if the marks are equal to 60.

Dim sngMarks As Single

sngMarks = 60

If sngMarks >= 80 Then

MsgBox "Excellent"

End If

If sngMarks >= 60 And sngMarks < 80 Then

MsgBox "Good"

End If

If sngMarks >= 40 And sngMarks < 60 Then

MsgBox "Average"

End If

If sngMarks < 40 Then

MsgBox "Poor"

End If

End Sub
```

Example 3

In this example, we will nest the If...Then...Else statements within a For...Next Loop.

```
Sub IfThenNesting()
```

'The user will need to enter 5 numbers. The compiler will add the even numbers and subtract the odd numbers.

Dim i As Integer, n As Integer, iEvenSum As Integer, iOddSum As Integer

```
For n = 1 To 5

i = InputBox("enter number")

If i Mod 2 = 0 Then

iEvenSum = iEvenSum + i

Else

iOddSum = iOddSum + i

End If

Next n

MsgBox "sum of even numbers is " & iEvenSum

MsgBox "sum of odd numbers is " & iOddSum

End Sub
```

Example 4

You can use the following options to test multiple variables using the If...Then statements.

Option 1: ElseIf Structure

```
Sub IfThen1()
```

'this procedure returns the message "Pass in maths and Fail in science"

```
Dim sngMaths As Single, sngScience As Single

sngMaths = 50

sngScience = 30

If sngMaths >= 40 And sngScience >= 40 Then

MsgBox "Pass in both maths and science"

ElseIf sngMaths >= 40 And sngScience < 40 Then

MsgBox "Pass in maths and Fail in science"

ElseIf sngMaths < 40 And sngScience >= 40 Then

MsgBox "Fail in maths and Pass in science"

Else

MsgBox "Fail in both maths and science"

End If

End Sub
```

Option 2: If...Then...Else Nesting

```
Sub IfThen2()

'this procedure returns the message "Pass in maths and Fail in science"

Dim sngMaths As Single, sngScience As Single

sngMaths = 50

sngScience = 30

If sngMaths >= 40 Then
```

```
If sngScience >= 40 Then

MsgBox "Pass in both maths and science"

Else

MsgBox "Pass in maths and Fail in science"

End If

Else

If sngScience >= 40 Then

MsgBox "Fail in maths and Pass in science"

Else

MsgBox "Fail in both maths and science"

End If

End If

End Sub
```

Option 3: Multiple If…Then Statements

As mentioned earlier, this may not be the best way to perform the operation.

```
Sub IfThen3()

'this procedure returns the message "Pass in maths and Fail in science"

Dim sngMaths As Single, sngScience As Single

sngMaths = 50

sngScience = 30
```

If sngMaths >= 40 And sngScience >= 40 Then

MsgBox "Pass in both maths and science"

End If

If sngMaths >= 40 And sngScience < 40 Then

MsgBox "Pass in maths and Fail in science"

End If

If sngMaths < 40 And sngScience >= 40 Then

MsgBox "Fail in maths and Pass in science"

End If

If sngMaths < 40 And sngScience < 40 Then

MsgBox "Fail in both maths and science"

End If

 End Sub

Example 5

In this example, we will use the If Not, If IsNumeric and IsEmpty functions in the Worksheet_Change event.

Private Sub Worksheet_Change(ByVal Target As Range)

'Using If IsEmpty, If Not and If IsNumeric (in If…Then statements) in the Worksheet_Change event.

'auto run a VBA code, when content of a worksheet cell changes, with the Worksheet_Change event.

On Error GoTo ErrHandler

Application.EnableEvents = False

'if target cell is empty post change, nothing will happen

If IsEmpty(Target) Then

Application.EnableEvents = True

Exit Sub

End If

'using If Not statement with the Intersect Method to determine if Target cell(s) is within specified range of "B1:B20"

If Not Intersect(Target, Range("B1:B20")) Is Nothing Then

'if target cell is changed to a numeric value

If IsNumeric(Target) Then

'changes the target cell color to yellow

Target.Interior.Color = RGB(255, 255, 0)

End If

End If

Application.EnableEvents = True

ErrHandler:

   Application.EnableEvents = True

   Exit Sub

End Sub

Using the Not Operator

When you use the Not operator on any Boolean expression, the compiler will reverse the true value with the false value and vice versa. The Not operator will always reverse the logic in any conditional statement. In the example above, If Not Intersect(Target, Range("B1:B20")) Is Nothing Then means If Intersect(Target, Range("B1:B20")) Is Not Nothing Then or If Intersect(Target, Range("B1:B20")) Is Something Then. In simple words, this means that the condition should not be true if the range falls or intersects between the range ("B1:B20").

Single Line If...Then...Else Statements

If you are writing a short or simple code, you should use the single-line syntax. If you wish to distinguish between the singly-line and multiple-line syntax, you should look at the block of code that succeeds the Then keyword. If there is nothing succeeding the Then keyword, the block of code is multiple-line. Otherwise, it is a single-line code.

The syntax for Single-line statements is as follows:

If condition Then statements Else else_statements

These blocks of statements can also be nested in a single-line syntax within each other. You can insert the clause Else If in the code, which is similar to the ElseIf clause. You do not need to use the End If keywords in the single-syntax block of code since the program will automatically terminate.

Let us look at some examples where we will use the single-line syntax for the If...Then...Else statements.

If sngMarks > 80 Then MsgBox "Excellent Marks"

If sngMarks > 80 Then MsgBox "Excellent Marks" Else MsgBox "Not Excellent"

'add MsgBox title "Grading":

If sngMarks > 80 Then MsgBox "Excellent Marks", , "Grading"

'using logical operator And in the condition:

If sngMarks > 80 And sngAvg > 80 Then MsgBox "Both Marks & Average are Excellent" Else MsgBox "Not Excellent"

'nesting another If...Then statement:

If sngMarks > 80 Then If sngAvg > 80 Then MsgBox "Both Marks & Average are Excellent"

Example 1

```
Sub IfThenSingleLine1()

Dim sngMarks As Single

sngMarks = 85
```

'Execute multiple statements / codes after Then keyword. Code will return 3 messages: "Excellent Marks - 85 on 90"; "Keep it up!" and "94.44% marks".

```
If sngMarks = 85 Then MsgBox "Excellent Marks - 85 on 90": MsgBox "Keep it up!": MsgBox Format(85 / 90 * 100, "0.00") & "% marks"

End Sub
```

Example 2

```
Sub IfThenSingleLine1()

Dim sngMarks As Single

sngMarks = 85
```

'Execute multiple statements / codes after Then keyword. Code will return 3 messages: "Excellent Marks - 85 on 90"; "Keep it up!" and "94.44% marks".

If sngMarks = 85 Then MsgBox "Excellent Marks - 85 on 90": MsgBox "Keep it up!": MsgBox Format(85 / 90 * 100, "0.00") & "% marks"

End Sub

Example 3

Sub IfThenSingleLine2()

Dim sngMarks As Single, sngAvg As Single

sngMarks = 85

sngAvg = 75

'nesting If...Then statements. Code will return the message: "Marks are Excellent, but Average is not"

If sngMarks > 80 Then If sngAvg > 80 Then MsgBox "Both Marks & Average are Excellent" Else MsgBox "Marks are Excellent, but Average is not" Else MsgBox "Marks are not Excellent"

End Sub

Example 4

Sub IfThenSingleLine3()

Dim sngMarks As Single

sngMarks = 65

'using the keywords Else If (in single-line syntax), similar to ElseIf (in multiple-line syntax). Procedure will return the message: "Marks are Good".

If sngMarks > 80 Then MsgBox "Marks are Excellent" Else If sngMarks >= 60 Then MsgBox "Marks are Good" Else If sngMarks >= 40 Then MsgBox "Marks are Average" Else MsgBox "Marks are Poor"

End Sub

Select…Case Statement

The Select…Case statement will execute statements or a block of code depending on whether some conditions have been met. It will evaluate an expression and executes one of the many blocks of code depending on the result of the expression. This statement is similar to the If…The…Else statement.

Syntax

Select Case expression

Case expression_value_1

statements_1

Case expression_value_n

statements_n

Case Else

else_statements

End Select

Expression

This can be a range, field or a variable. The expression can be expressed by using a VBA function -> as "rng.HasFormula" or "IsNumeric(rng)" where the 'rng' is the range variable. The expression can return a String value, Boolean Value, Numeric Value or any other data type. It is important that you specify the expression. It is the value of the expression that the compiler will test and compare with each case in the

Select…Case statement. When the values match, the compiler will execute the block of code under the matching Case.

Expression_value

The data type of the expression_value should be the same as the expression or a similar data type. The compiler will compare the value of the expression against the expression_value in each case. If it finds a match, the block of code under the case or the statements will be executed. You must specify at least one expression_value, and the compiler will test the expression against these values in the order they are mentioned in. The expression_values are similar to a list of conditions where the condition must be met for the relevant block of code to be executed.

Statements

The compiler will execute the block of code or statements under a specific case if the value of the expression and the expression_value are the same.

Case Else -> expression_value

When the compiler matches the value of the expression to the expression_value, it will execute the block of code under that case. It will not check the value of the expression against the remaining expression_value. If the compiler does not find a match against any expression_value, it will move to the Case Else clause. The statements under this clause are executed. You do not have to use this clause when you write your code.

Else_statements

As mentioned earlier, the else_statements are included in the Case Else section of the code. If the compiler cannot match the value of the expression to any expression_value, it will execute these statements.

End Select

These keywords terminate the Select...Case block of statements. You must mention these keywords at the end of the Select...Case statements.

Let us look at an example of the Select...Case statements.

```
Sub selectCase1()

'making strAge equivalent to "young" will return the message "Less than 40 years"

Dim strAge As String

strAge = "young"

Select Case strAge

Case "senior citizen"

MsgBox "Over 60 years"

Case "middle age"

MsgBox "Between 40 to 59 years"

Case "young"

MsgBox "Less than 40 years"

Case Else

MsgBox "Invalid"

End Select

End Sub
```

Using the To Keyword

You can use the To keyword to specify the upper and lower range of all matching values in the expression_value section of the Select...Case statements. The value on the left side of the To keyword should either be less than or equal to the value on the right side of the To keyword. You can also specify the range for a specified set of characters.

Let us look at an example.

```
Sub selectCaseTo()

'entering marks as 69 will return the message "Average"; entering marks as 101 will return the message "Out of Range"

Dim iMarks As Integer

iMarks = InputBox("Enter marks")

Select Case iMarks

Case 70 To 100

MsgBox "Good"

Case 40 To 69

MsgBox "Average"

Case 0 To 39

MsgBox "Failed"

Case Else

MsgBox "Out of Range"

End Select

End Sub
```

Using the Is Keyword

You can use the Is keyword if you want to include a comparison operator like <>, ==, <=, >=, < or >. If you do not include the Is keyword, the compiler will automatically include it. Let us look at the example below.

```
Sub selectCaseIs()

'if sngTemp equals 39.5, returned message is "Moderately Hot"

Dim sngTemp As Single

sngTemp = 39.5

Select Case sngTemp

Case Is >= 40

MsgBox "Extremely Hot"

Case Is >= 25

MsgBox "Moderately Hot"

Case Is >= 0

MsgBox "Cool Weather"

Case Is < 0

MsgBox "Extremely Cold"

End Select

End Sub
```

Using a comma

You can include multiple ranges or expressions in the Case clause. These ranges and expressions can be separated with a comma. The comma acts like the OR operator. You can also specify multiple expressions and ranges for character strings. Let us look at the example below.

Example 1

```
Sub selectCaseMultiple_1()

'if alpha equates to "Hello," the returned message is "Odd Number or Hello"

Dim alpha As Variant

alpha = "Hello"

Select Case alpha

Case a, e, i, o, u

MsgBox "Vowels"

Case 2, 4, 6, 8

MsgBox "Even Number"

Case 1, 3, 5, 7, 9, "Hello"

MsgBox "Odd Number or Hello"

Case Else

MsgBox "Out of Range"

End Select

End Sub
```

Example 2

In this example, we are comparing the strings "apples" to "grapes." The compiler will determine the value between "apples" and "grapes" and will use the default comparison method binary.

Sub SelectCaseMultiple_OptionCompare_NotSpecified()

'Option Compare is NOT specified and therefore text comparison will be case-sensitive

'bananas will return the message "Text between apples and grapes, or specifically mangoes, or the numbers 98 or 99"; oranges will return the message "Out of Range"; Apples will return the message "Out of Range."

```
Dim var As Variant, strResult As String

var = InputBox("Enter")

Select Case var

Case 1 To 10, 11 To 20: strResult = "Number is between 1 and
20"

Case "apples" To "grapes," "mangoes," 98, 99: strResult = "Text
between apples and grapes, or specifically mangoes, or the
numbers 98 or 99"

Case Else: strResult = "Out of Range"

End Select

MsgBox strResult

End Sub
```

Nesting

You can nest the Select...Case block of code or statements within VBA loops, If...Then...Else statements and within a Select...Case block. There is no limit on the number of cases you can include in the code. If you are nesting a Select...Case within another Select...Case, it should be a complete block by itself and also terminate with its End Select.

Example 1

Sub selectCaseNested1()

Check if a range is empty; and if not empty, whether it has a numeric value and if numeric then if also has a formula; and if not numeric then what is the text length.

Dim rng As Range, iLength As Integer

Set rng = ActiveSheet.Range("A1")

Select Case IsEmpty(rng)

Case True

MsgBox rng.Address & " is empty"

Case Else

Select Case IsNumeric(rng)

Case True

MsgBox rng.Address & " has a numeric value"

Select Case rng.HasFormula

Case True

MsgBox rng.Address & " also has a formula"

End Select

Case Else

iLength = Len(rng)

MsgBox rng.Address & " has a Text length of " & iLength

End Select

End Select

End Sub

Example 2

```
Function StringManipulation(str As String) As String
```

'This code customizes a string text as follows:

'1. removes numericals from a text string;

'2. removes leading, trailing & inbetween spaces (leaves single space between words);

'3. adds space (if not present) after each exclamation, comma, full stop and question mark;

'4. capitalizes the very first letter of the string and the first letter of a word after each exclamation, full stop and question mark;

```
 Dim iTxtLen As Integer, iStrLen As Integer, n As Integer, i As Integer, ansiCode As Integer

    '-------------------------
```

'REMOVE NUMERICALS

'chr(48) to chr(57) represent numericals 0 to 9 in ANSI/ASCII character codes

For i = 48 To 57

'remove all numericals from the text string using vba Replace function:

str = Replace(str, Chr(i), "")

Next i

'--------------------------

'REMOVE LEADING, TRAILING & INBETWEEN SPACES (LEAVE SINGLE SPACE BETWEEN WORDS)

'use the worksheet TRIM function. Note: the TRIM function removes space character with ANSI code 32, does not remove the nonbreaking space character with ANSI code 160

str = Application.Trim(str)

'--------------------------

'ADD SPACE (IF NOT PRESENT) AFTER EACH EXCLAMATION, COMMA, DOT AND QUESTION MARK:

'set variable value to string length:

iTxtLen = Len(str)

For n = iTxtLen To 1 Step -1

'Chr(32) returns space; Chr(33) returns exclamation; Chr(44) returns comma; Chr(46) returns full stop; Chr(63) returns question mark;

If Mid(str, n, 1) = Chr(33) Or Mid(str, n, 1) = Chr(44) Or Mid(str, n, 1) = Chr(46) Or Mid(str, n, 1) = Chr(63) Then 'check if space is not present:

```
If Mid(str, n + 1, 1) <> Chr(32) Then
```

'using Mid & Right functions to add space - note that current string length is used:

```
str = Mid(str, 1, n) & Chr(32) & Right(str, iTxtLen - n)
```

'update string length - increments by 1 after adding a space (character):

```
iTxtLen = iTxtLen + 1

End If

End If

Next n
```

'-------------------------

'DELETE SPACE (IF PRESENT) BEFORE EACH EXCLAMATION, COMMA, DOT & QUESTION MARK:

'reset variable value to string length:

```
iTxtLen = Len(str)

For n = iTxtLen To 1 Step -1
```

'Chr(32) returns space; Chr(33) returns exclamation; Chr(44) returns comma; Chr(46) returns full stop; Chr(63) returns question mark;

```
If Mid(str, n, 1) = Chr(33) Or Mid(str, n, 1) = Chr(44) Or Mid(str, n, 1) = Chr(46) Or Mid(str, n, 1) = Chr(63) Then
```

'check if space is present:

```
If Mid(str, n - 1, 1) = Chr(32) Then
```

'using the worksheet Replace function to delete a space:

str = Application.Replace(str, n - 1, 1, "")

'omit rechecking the same character again - position of n shifts (decreases by 1) due to deleting a space character:

n = n - 1

End If

End If

Next n

'---------------------------

'CAPITALIZE LETTERS:

'capitalize the very first letter of the string and the first letter of a word after each exclamation, full stop and question mark, while all other letters are lower case

iStrLen = Len(str)

For i = 1 To iStrLen

'determine the ANSI code of each character in the string

ansiCode = Asc(Mid(str, i, 1))

Select Case ansiCode

'97 to 122 are the ANSI codes equating to small cap letters "a" to "z"

Case 97 To 122

If i > 2 Then

'capitalizes a letter whose position is 2 characters after (1 character after, will be the space character added earlier) an exclamation, full stop and question mark:

```vb
If Mid(str, i - 2, 1) = Chr(33) Or Mid(str, i - 2, 1) = Chr(46) Or
Mid(str, i - 2, 1) = Chr(63) Then

Mid(str, i, 1) = UCase(Mid(str, i, 1))

End If

'capitalize first letter of the string:

ElseIf i = 1 Then

Mid(str, i, 1) = UCase(Mid(str, i, 1))

End If

'if capital letter, skip to next character (ie. next i):

Case Else

GoTo skip

End Select

skip:

Next i

'-------------------------

'manipulated string:

StringManipulation = str

End Function

Sub Str_Man()

'specify text string to manipulate & get manipulated string

Dim strText As String

'specify the text string, which is required to be manipulated
```

strText = ActiveSheet.Range("A1").Value

'the manipulated text string is entered in range A5 of the active sheet, on running the procedure:

ActiveSheet.Range("A5").Value = StringManipulation(strText)

End Sub

Go To Statement

You can use the Go To statement to move to a different section of the code or jump a line in the procedure. There are two parts to the Go To statement:

1. The GoTo keywords that are followed by an identifier, also known as the Label.

2. The Label which is followed by a colon and the line of code or a few statements.

If the value of the expression satisfies the condition, the compiler will move to a separate line of code that is indicated in the GoTo statement. You can avoid this statement and use the If…Then…Else statement. The Go To function makes the code unreadable and confusing.

Select…Case Statements Versus the If…Then…Else Statements

The Select…Case and If…Then…Else statements are both conditional statements. In each of these statements either one or more conditions are tested and the compiler will execute the block of code depending on what the result of the evaluation is.

The difference between the two statements is that in the Select…Case statement only one condition is evaluated at a time. The variable that is to be evaluated is initialized or declared in the Select Case expression. The multiple case statements will specify the different values that the variable can take. In the If…Then…Else statement, multiple conditions can be evaluated and the code for different conditions can be executed at the same time.

The Select...Case statement will only test a single variable for several values while the If...Then...Else statement will test multiple variables for different values. In this sense, the If...Then... Else statement is more flexible since you can test multiple variables for different conditions.

If you are testing a large number of conditions, you should avoid using the If...Then...Else statements since they may appear confusing. These statements can also make it difficult for you to read the code.

Chapter Five

Working With Strings

Strings are an integral part of VBA, and every programmer will need to work with strings when he or she begins to automate functions using VBA. There are different types of manipulations that one can do on strings including

- Extracting some parts of a string

- Comparing different strings

- Converting a number into a string

- Formatting dates to include weekdays

- Finding the characters in a string

- Removing the blanks in a string

- Parsing the string into an array

There are many functions in VBA that you can use to perform these tasks. This chapter will act as a guide on how you can work with strings in VBA. There are some simple examples in the book that you can practice.

Points to Remember

There are two points that you need to keep in mind when you work with strings.

Original String Does Not Change

You must remember that the original string function does not change when you perform some operations on strings. VBA returns a new string with all the changes you have made to it. If you want to make a change to the original string, you should assign the result of the function to the original string. We will cover this concept later in this chapter.

Comparing Two Strings

There are some string functions like Instr() and StrComp() that allow you to include the **Compare** parameter. This parameter works in the following way:

- **vbTextCompare**: The upper and lower case letters in the string are considered the same.

- **vbBinaryCompare**: The upper and lower case letters in the string are treated differently.

Let us look at the following example to see how you can use the Compare parameter in the StrComp() function.

```
Sub Comp1()

    ' Prints 0 if the strings do not match

    Debug.Print StrComp("MARoon", "Maroon",
vbTextCompare)

    ' Prints 1 if the strings do not match

    Debug.Print StrComp("Maroon", "MAROON",
vbBinaryCompare)

End Sub
```

Instead of using the same parameter every time, you can use the Option Compare. This parameter is defined at the top of any module, and a function that includes the parameter Compare will use this setting as its default. You can use the Option Compare in the following ways:

Option Compare Text

This option makes uses the vbTextCompare as the default compare argument.

```
Option Compare Text

Sub Comp2()

    ' Strings match - uses vbCompareText as Compare argument

    Debug.Print StrComp("ABC", "abc")

    Debug.Print StrComp("DEF", "def")

End Sub
```

Option Compare Binary

This option uses the vbBinaryCompare as the default compare argument.

```
Option Compare Binary

    Sub Comp2()

        ' Strings do not match - uses vbCompareBinary as Compare argument

        Debug.Print StrComp("ABC", "abc")

        Debug.Print StrComp("DEF", "def")

    End Sub
```

If you do not use the Option Compare statement, VBA uses Option Compare Binary as the default. Please keep these points in mind when we look at the individual string functions.

Appending Strings

You can use the & operator to append strings in VBA. Let us look at some examples of how you can use this operator to append strings.

```
Sub Append()

    Debug.Print "ABC" & "DEF"

    Debug.Print "Jane" & " " & "Smith"

    Debug.Print "Long " & 22

    Debug.Print "Double " & 14.99

    Debug.Print "Date " & #12/12/2015#

End Sub
```

In the example above, there are different types of data that we have converted to string using the quotes. You will see that the plus operator can also be used to append strings in some programs. The difference between using the & operator and + operator is that the latter will only work with string data types. If you use it with any other data type, you will get an error message.

```
    ' You will get the following error:  "Type Mismatch"

    Debug.Print "Long " + 22
```

If you want to use a complex function to append strings, you should use the Format function which is described later in this chapter.

Extracting Parts of a String

In this section, we will look at some functions that you can use to extract information or data from strings.

You can use the Right, Left and Mid functions to extract the necessary parts in a string. These functions are simple to use. The Right function reads the sentence from the right, the Left function reads the sentence from the left and the Mid function will read the sentence from the point that you specify.

```vba
Sub UseLeftRightMid()

    Dim sCustomer As String

    sCustomer = "John Thomas Smith"

    Debug.Print Left(sCustomer, 4) ' This will print John

    Debug.Print Right(sCustomer, 5) ' This will print Smith

    Debug.Print Left(sCustomer, 11) ' This will print John Thomas

    Debug.Print Right(sCustomer, 12) ' This will print Thomas Smith

    Debug.Print Mid(sCustomer, 1, 4) ' This will print John

    Debug.Print Mid(sCustomer, 6, 6) ' This will print Thomas

    Debug.Print Mid(sCustomer, 13, 5) ' This will print Smith

End Sub
```

As mentioned earlier, the string functions in VBA do not change the original string but return a new string as the result. In the following example, you will see that the string "FullName" remains unchanged even after the use of the Left function.

```vba
Sub UsingLeftExample()

    Dim Fullname As String

    Fullname = "John Smith"

    Debug.Print "Firstname is: "; Left(Fullname, 4)
```

' The original string remains unchanged

Debug.Print "Fullname is: "; Fullname

End Sub

If you wish to make a change to the original string, you will need to assign the return value of the function to the original string.

```
Sub ChangingString()

    Dim name As String

    name = "John Smith"

    ' The return value of the function is assigned to the original
    string

    name = Left(name, 4)

    Debug.Print "Name is: "; name

End Sub
```

Searching in a String

InStr and InStrRev are two functions that you can use in VBA to search for substrings within a string. If the compiler can find the substring in the string, the position of the string is returned. This position is the index from where the string starts. If the substring is not found, the compiler will return zero. If the original string and substring are null, the value null is returned.

InStr

Description of Parameters

The function is written as follows:

InStr() Start[Optional], String1, String2, Compare[Optional]

1. **Start**: This number specified where the compiler should start looking for the substring within the actual string. The default option is one.

2. **String1**: This is the original string.

3. **String2**: This is the substring that you want the compiler to search for.

4. **Compare**: This is the method we looked at in the first part of this chapter.

The Use and Examples

This function will return the first position in the string where the substring is found. Let us look at the following example:

Sub FindSubString()

  Dim name As String

  name = "John Smith"

  ' This will return the number 3 which indicates the position of the first h

  Debug.Print InStr(name, "h")

  ' This will return the number 10 which indicates the position of the first h starting from position 4

  Debug.Print InStr(4, name, "h")

  ' This will return 8

  Debug.Print InStr(name, "it")

  ' This will return 6

  Debug.Print InStr(name, "Smith")

' This will return zero since the string "SSS" was not found

Debug.Print InStr(name, "SSS")

End Sub

InStrRev

Description of Parameters

The function is written as follows:

InStrRev() StringCheck, StringMatch, Start[Optional], Compare[Optional]

1. **StringCheck**: This is the string that you need to search for.

2. **StringMatch**: This is the string the compiler should look for.

3. **Start**: This number specified where the compiler should start looking for the substring within the actual string. The default option is one.

4. **Compare**: This is the method we looked at in the first part of this chapter.

The Use and Examples

This function is the same as the InStr function except that is starts the search from the end of the original string. You must note that the position that the compiler returns is the position from the start of the sentence. Therefore, if the substring is available only once in the sentence, the InStr() and InStrRev() functions return the same value.

Let us look at some examples of the InStrRev function.

Sub UsingInstrRev()

Dim name As String

name = "John Smith"

' Both functions will return 1 which is the position of the only J

    Debug.Print InStr(name, "J")

    Debug.Print InStrRev(name, "J")

' This will return 10 which indicates the second h

    Debug.Print InStrRev(name, "h")

' This will return the number 3 and it indicates the first h as searches from position 9

    Debug.Print InStrRev(name, "h", 9)

' This will return 1

    Debug.Print InStrRev(name, "John")

    End Sub

You should use the InStr and InStrRev functions when you want to perform basic searches in strings. If you want to extract some text from a string, the process is slightly complicated.

Removing Blanks

In VBA, you can use the trim functions to remove blanks or spaces either at the start or end of a string.

The Use and Examples

1. **Trim**: Removes the spaces from both the right and left of a string.

2. **LTrim**: Removes the spaces only from the left of the string.

3. **RTrim**: Removes the spaces from the right of the string.

```
Sub TrimStr()

    Dim name As String

    name = "  John Smith  "

    ' Will print "John Smith  "

    Debug.Print LTrim(name)

    ' Will print "  John Smith"

    Debug.Print RTrim(name)

    ' Will print "John Smith"

    Debug.Print Trim(name)

End Sub
```

Length of a String

You can use Len to return the length of the string since it is a simple function. This function will return the number of characters in the string. If you use different numeric data types like long, the function will return the number of bytes in the string.

```
    Sub GetLen()

        Dim name As String

        name = "John Smith"

        ' This will print 10

        Debug.Print Len("John Smith")

        ' This will print 3

        Debug.Print Len("ABC")
```

132

' This will print 4 since the numeric data type Long is 4 bytes in size

```
Dim total As Long

Debug.Print Len(total)
```

End Sub

Reversing a String

The StrReverse function is another easy function to use. This will return the original string with the characters reversed.

```
Sub RevStr()

    Dim s As String

    s = "Jane Smith"

    ' This will print htimS enaJ

    Debug.Print StrReverse(s)

End Sub
```

Comparing Strings

You can use the function StrComp to compare two strings.

Description of Parameters

The function is written as follows:

StrComp() String1, String2, Compare[Optional]

1. **String1**: The first string that needs to be compared.

2. **String2**: The second string that needs to be compared.

3. **Compare**: This is the method we looked at in the first part of this chapter.

The Use and Examples

Let us look at some examples of how to use the StrComp function:

```
Sub UsingStrComp()

    ' This will return 0

    Debug.Print StrComp("ABC", "ABC", vbTextCompare)

    ' This will return 1

    Debug.Print StrComp("ABCD", "ABC", vbTextCompare)

    ' This will return -1

    Debug.Print StrComp("ABC", "ABCD", vbTextCompare)

    ' This will return Null

    Debug.Print StrComp(Null, "ABCD", vbTextCompare)

End Sub
```

Comparing Strings Using Operators

VBA allows you to use the equal to sign to compare two strings. The differences between the StrComp and equal to sign are:

- The equal to sign will return either true or false.

- You cannot combine a Compare parameter with the equal sign since it will only use the Option Compare setting.

Let us look at a few examples where we use the equal to sign to compare two strings.

Option Compare Text

    Sub CompareUsingEquals()

      ' This will return true

      Debug.Print "ABC" = "ABC"

      ' This will return True since the compare text parameter is at the start of the program

      Debug.Print "ABC" = "abc"

      ' This will return false

      Debug.Print "ABCD" = "ABC"

      ' This will return false

      Debug.Print "ABC" = "ABCD"

      ' This will return null

      Debug.Print Null = "ABCD"

    End Sub

To see if two strings are not equal, you must use the "<>" operator. This operator performs a function that is opposite to the equal to sign.

Option Compare Text

    Sub CompareWithNotEqual()

      ' This will return false

      Debug.Print "ABC" <> "ABC"

      ' This will return false since the Compare Text parameter is at the start of the program

      Debug.Print "ABC" <> "abc"

' This will return true

Debug.Print "ABCD" <> "ABC"

' This will return true

Debug.Print "ABC" <> "ABCD"

' This will return null

Debug.Print Null <> "ABCD"

End Sub

Comparing Strings Using Pattern Matching

Pattern matching is a VBA technique that helps you determine if a string has a specific pattern of characters. For instance, there are times when you need to check if a customer number has 3 numeric values and 3 alphabetic characters or if a specific string has the letters ABC followed by a set of numbers or characters. If the compiler deems that the string matches the pattern, it will return the value "True," otherwise, it will return the value "False."

Pattern matching is similar to the Format function. This means that you can use pattern matching in multiple ways. In this section, we will look at some examples that will help you understand how the pattern matching technique works. This will cover the common uses of pattern matching. Let us take the following string: [abc][!def]]?#X*

Let us look at how this string will work:

1. [abc]: This will represent a character – a, b or c.

2. [!def]: This will represent a character that is not d, e or f.

3. ?: This will represent any character.

4. #: This will represent any digit.

136

5. X: This represents the character X.

6. *: This means that the string is followed by more characters or zero.

Therefore, this is a valid string.

Now, let us consider the following string: apY6X.

1. a: This character is one of a, b and c.

2. p: This is not a character that is d, e or f.

3. Y: This is any character.

4. 6: This is a digit.

5. X: This is the letter X.

You can now say that the pattern for both strings is the same.

Let us look at a code that will show you a variety of results when you use the same pattern:

```
Sub Patterns()

    ' This will print true

    Debug.Print 1; "apY6X" Like "[abc][!def]?#X*"

    ' This will print true since any combination is valid after X

    Debug.Print 2; "apY6Xsf34FAD" Like "[abc][!def]?#X*"

    ' This will print false since the character is not a, b or c

    Debug.Print 3; "dpY6X" Like "[abc][!def]?#X*"

    ' This will print false since the character is one of d, e and f

    Debug.Print 4; "aeY6X" Like "[abc][!def]?#X*"
```

' This will print false since the character at 4 should be a digit.

    Debug.Print 5; "apYAX" Like "[abc][!def]?#X*"

' This will print false since the character at position 5 should be X.

    Debug.Print 1; "apY6Z" Like "[abc][!def]?#X*"

End Sub

Replacing Part of a String

You should use the replace function when you want to replace a substring in a string using another substring. This function will replace all the instances where the substrings are found.

Description of Parameters

The function is written as follows:

Replace() Expression, Find, Replace, Start[Optional], Count[Optional], Compare[Optional]

1. Expression: This is the original string.

2. Find: This is the substring that you want to replace in the Expression string.

3. Replace: This is the substring you want to replace the Find substring with.

4. Start: This is the start position of the string. The position is taken as 1 by default.

5. Count: This is the number of substitutions you want to make. The default is one, which means that all the Find substrings are replaced with the Replace substring.

6. Compare: This is the method we looked at in the first part of this chapter.

The Use and Examples

In the following code, we will look at some examples of how to use the Replace function.

```
Sub ReplaceExamples()

    ' To replace all the question marks in the string with semi colons.

    Debug.Print Replace("A?B?C?D?E", "?", ";")

    ' To replace Smith with Jones

    Debug.Print Replace("Peter Smith,Ann Smith", "Smith", "Jones")

    ' To replace AX with AB

    Debug.Print Replace("ACD AXC BAX", "AX", "AB")

End Sub
```

The output will be as follows:

A;B;C;D;E

Peter Jones,Sophia Jones

ACD ABC BAB

In the next block of code, we will use the Count optional parameter to determine the number of substitutions you want to make. For instance, if you set up Count equal to one, it means that you want the compiler to only replace the first occurrence of the Find string.

```
Sub ReplaceCount()
```

' To replace only the first question mark

Debug.Print Replace("A?B?C?D?E", "?", ";", Count:=1)

' To replace the first two question marks

Debug.Print Replace("A?B?C?D?E", "?", ";", Count:=2)

End Sub

The output will be as follows:

A;B?C?D?E

A;B;C?D?E

You can return a part of the string if you use the Start optional parameter. The compiler will return the part of the string from the position that you specify in the Start parameter. When you use this operator, it will ignore all the words or the part of the string before the start position.

Sub ReplacePartial()

' This will use the original string from the position 4

Debug.Print Replace("A?B?C?D?E", "?", ";", Start:=4)

' This will use the original string from the position 8

Debug.Print Replace("AA?B?C?D?E", "?", ";", Start:=8)

' There are no items that will be replaced, but it will return the last two values

Debug.Print Replace("ABCD", "X", "Y", Start:=3)

End Sub

The output will be as follows:

;C;D;E

140

;E

CD

There may be times when you want to replace only the lower or upper case letters in a string. At such times, you can use the Compare parameter. This is a parameter that can be used in many string functions. To understand this better, you should refer to the section above.

```
Sub ReplaceCase()

    ' This will only replace the capitalized A's

    Debug.Print Replace("AaAa", "A", "X",
Compare:=vbBinaryCompare)

    ' This will replace all the A's

    Debug.Print Replace("AaAa", "A", "X",
Compare:=vbTextCompare)

End Sub
```

The output is as follows:

XaXa

XXXX

Multiple Replaces

You can nest the calls if you want to replace more than one value in a string. Let us look at the following example where we will replace the X and Y with A and B respectively.

```
Sub ReplaceMulti()

    Dim newString As String

    ' Replace the A with X
```

```
newString = Replace("ABCD ABDN", "A", "X")

' Replace the B with Y in the new string

newString = Replace(newString, "B", "Y")

Debug.Print newString

End Sub
```

In the example below, we will make a few changes to the code above to perform this task. The return value of the first function is used as the argument or the original string for the second replacement.

```
Sub ReplaceMultiNested()

Dim newString As String

' To replace A with X and B with Y

newString = Replace(Replace("ABCD ABDN", "A", "X"),
"B", "Y")

Debug.Print newString

End Sub
```

The result of these replacements will be XYCD XYDN.

Chapter Six

Error Handling and Debugging

Error handling is a common programming practice where the programmer should anticipate and code for error conditions, which may arise when he or she runs the program. You will come across three errors – user entry data errors where the user enters a negative number instead of a positive number, run time errors which occur when VBA cannot execute a program statement and compiler errors where the programmer has not declared a variable. We will only worry about the run time errors in this chapter since the other two errors are easy for a programmer to solve. Typical errors include those where VBA is attempting to access a worksheet or workbook that is non-existent or attempting to divide a number by zero. The code in this chapter will use try to divide a number by zero since we want to raise an error.

You should include as many checks as you can when you write the code to ensure that you do not come across any run time errors when you execute the code. This includes ensuring that the worksheets and workbooks being referred to in the code are all present and the names are defined. When you constantly check the application when you write the code, you can ensure that the macro is stable. This is better than to detect an error when your application is running.

If a run time error occurs and you do not have a code written to handle the errors, VBA will display the run time error dialog box. When the application is in the development stage, you can welcome these errors. If the application is at the final stage or in the production environment, you cannot expect to face these errors. The goal of an error handling code is to ensure that you identify the errors at run time and then correct them immediately. The goal should be to prevent the occurrence of any unhandled errors.

In this chapter, we will refer to Property procedure, Function and Sub as procedure and the words exit statement will mean Exit Property, Exit Function and Exit Sub. The words end statement will mean End Property, End Function, End Sub and End.

The On Error Statement

The heart of every error handling process in VBA is the On Error statement. When a run time error occurs, this statement will tell VBA what it must do to counter the error. The On Error statement takes the following forms:

1. On Error Goto 0

2. On Error Resume Next

3. On Error Goto <label>:

On Error Goto o is the default in VBA. This statement indicates that VBA should always display the standard run time error dialog box if it encounters a run time error when it executes the code. This will give you a chance to enter the debug mode and check the code. Alternatively, you can terminate the code. The On Error Goto o is the same as not including an error handling statement in your code. The error will prompt VBA to display the standard window.

The On Error Resume Next is the most misused and commonly used form. This statement will instruct VBA to ignore the line of code that has the error and move to the next line of code. You must remember that this statement does not fix the code in any way. It will only tell VBA to act as if there was no error in the code. This error can have a negative effect on the code. It is important that you test your code for any errors and then take appropriate actions to solve those errors. You can do this by executing the appropriate code when the value of Err.Number is not zero. For instance,

```
On Error Resume Next

N = 1 / 0    ' cause an error

If Err.Number <> 0 Then

    N = 1

End If
```

In the above code, we are assigning the value of 1/0 to a variable N. This is an incorrect approach, therefore VBA will raise the Division By Zero Error (Error 11). The code will continue to execute since we have used the On Error Resume Next statement. The statement will assign a value to the variable N after it tests the value of Err.Number.

The third form is the On Error Goto <lable>. This statement will tell VBA that it needs to execute the line of code after a specific line label if an error occurs. When the error occurs, VBA will ignore every line of code between the error line and the specified line label, including any loop statements.

```
On Error Goto ErrHandler:

N = 1 / 0    ' cause an error

'

' more code

'

Exit Sub

ErrHandler:

' error handling code

Resume Next

End Sub
```

Enabled and Active Error Handlers

When the On Error statement is executed, VBA will enable an error handler. It is important to remember that VBA will only enable on error handler at any given point, and it will behave according to that error handler. VBA will execute the code in this error handler when any error occurs. The execution is transferred to a different location using the On Error Goto <label>: statement. The code in the error handler should either resume execution in the main program or fix the error in the program. You an also use the error handler to terminate the execution of the program. You cannot use it like the second form of the On Error statement to skip a few lines. For example, the code below will not function correctly:

On Error GoTo Err1:

Debug.Print 1 / 0

' more code

Err1:

On Error GoTo Err2:

Debug.Print 1 / 0

' more code

Err2:

The execution of code transfers to Err1 when the first error occurs. Since the error handler is active when the next error occurs, the On Error statement will not trap the error.

The Resume Statement

The Resume statement will instruct VBA to resume the execution of the code at a specific point the code. You should use the Resume statement only in the error handling blocks of code. If you use it in another part of the program, it will cause an error. You should not use the Goto statement to direct the code execution out of the error handling section of code. If you do this, you will encounter some strange problems with error handlers.

There are three syntactic forms that the Resume statement takes:

1. Resume

2. Resume Next

3. Resume <label>

When Resume is used alone, it will instruct VBA to resume the execution of the program at the line of code that has the error. If you use this, you must ensure that the error handling code or block can fix the problem. Otherwise, the code will enter a loop that is endless since it will be jumping between the error handling block and the line that caused the error. In the example below, we will try to activate a worksheet that does not exist. VBA will give you an error (Subscript Out Of Range) and will immediately jump to the error handling code. This code will then create a sheet and solve the problems. The execution will then resume at the line of code that caused the error.

```
On Error GoTo ErrHandler:

Worksheets("NewSheet").Activate

Exit Sub

ErrHandler:

If Err.Number = 9 Then

    ' sheet does not exist, so create it

    Worksheets.Add.Name = "NewSheet"

    ' go back to the line of code that caused the problem

    Resume

End If
```

147

The second form of the Resume is Resume Next. This statement will instruct VBA to execute the line of code that immediately follows the line that caused the error. The following code sets a value to the variable N and it causes an error. The error handling code will assign the variable N a value 1, and will continue to execute the remainder of the program.

On Error GoTo ErrHandler:

N = 1 / 0

Debug.Print N

Exit Sub

ErrHandler:

N = 1

' go back to the line following the error

Resume Next

The third form is the Resume <label> form. This is similar to the On Error Goto <label> statement. The statement will instruct VBA to execute the code from the line label. This means that it will skip the part of the code where there is an error. For instance,

On Error GoTo ErrHandler:

N = 1 / 0

'

' code that is skipped if an error occurs

'

Label1:

'

```
' more code to execute

'

Exit Sub

ErrHandler:

' go back to the line at Label1:

Resume Label1:
```

Every form of the Resume statement will either clear or reset the error object.

Error Handling With Multiple Procedures

You do not need to include an error code in every procedure. If an error occurs while running a program, VBA will use the last On Error statement and act accordingly. If the code that is causing the error is in the same procedure as the On Error statements, the error is handled in the ways mentioned above. If the procedure does not have an error handling code, VBA will need to go back to the procedure and proceed backward until it reaches the line with the incorrect code. For example, a procedure A calls B and B calls C, and only procedure A has an error handling code. If an error occurs in C, VBA will go back to the error handling code in procedure A. It will skip all the code in procedure B.

A Note of Caution

You may want to use the On Error Resume Next statement when you are dealing with errors. This is a bad coding practice since you cannot run the code without solving the errors. You have to remember that this statement does not skip errors but ignores them.

Chapter Seven

Mistakes to Avoid

I f you are reading this chapter, you will be familiar with Excel VBA. It is easy for anybody to make mistakes when they write a code in VBA. These mistakes will cost you greatly. This chapter lists the common mistakes that most VBA amateurs make.

Not Using Arrays

An interesting mistake that most VBA programmers make is that they try to process all the functions in a large nested loop. They filter the data down through the different rows and columns in the worksheet during the process of calculation. This method can work, but it can lead to performance troubles. If you have to perform the same function repeatedly, the efficiency of the macro will decrease. When you loop through the same column and you extract the values every single time, you are not only affecting the macro, but also affecting the processor. An efficient way to handle a list of numbers is to use an array.

If you have not used an array before, let me introduce it to you now. An array is a set of elements that have the same data type. Each element in the array is given an index. You must use this index to refer to the element in the array. An array can be defined by using the following statement: Dim MyArray (12) as Integer. This will create an array with 12 indices and variables that you will need to fill. Let us look at how a loop with an array will look like:

```
Sub Test1()

    Dim x As Integer
```

```
        intNumRows = Range("A2",
Range("A2").End(xldown)).Rows.Count

        Range("A2").Select

        For x = 1 To intNumRows

            arrMyArray(x-1) = Range("A" & str(x)).value

            ActiveCell.Offset(1, 0).Select

        Next

    End Sub
```

In this example, the code is processing through every cell in the range before it performs the calculation function.

Using .Select or .Activate

You do not have to always use the .Select or .Activate functions when you write code in VBA. You may want to use these functions since the Macro Recorder generates them. These functions are unnecessary for the following reasons:

- These functions may lead to the repainting of the screen. If you use the following function Sheets("Sheet1").Activate, Excel will redraw the screen so you can see Sheet1. This will lead to a slow macro.

- These functions will confuse users since you will be manipulating the workbook when the user is working on it. There are some users who will worry that they are being hacked.

You should use these functions only when you want to bring the user to a specific cell or worksheet. Otherwise, you should delete the line of code since it will be doing more harm than good.

Using Variant Type

Another mistake that most programmers make is to use one Type when they are actually using another. If you look at the following code, you will think that a, b and c are of the Long type. Well, that is incorrect since the variables a and b are of the Variant type. This means that they can be any data type, and can change from one type to another.

It is dangerous to have a variant type since it will become difficult for you to identify the bugs in your code. You should always avoid Variant types in VBA. There are some functions that will need the use of a Variant type, but you should avoid them if you can.

Not Using Application.ScreenUpdating = False

When you make a change to a cell or a group of cells in your code, Excel will need to repaint the screen to show the user the changes. This will make your macros slow. When you write a macro the next time, you should use the following lines of code:

```
Public Sub MakeCodeFaster()

    Application.ScreenUpdating = False


    ' Block of code

    ' This setting should always be reset back

    Application.ScreenUpdating = True

End Sub
```

Referencing the Worksheet Name with a String

People will refer to a worksheet using a String. Look at the following example:

```
Public Sub SheetReferenceExample()
```

```
Dim ws As Worksheet

Set ws = Sheets("Sheet1")

Debug.Print ws.Name

End Sub
```

This does seem harmless does it not? In most cases, it is harmless. Imagine that you give another person this workbook, and that person decides to rename the sheet to "Reprot." When he tries to run the macro, the macro will look for "Sheet1," which no longer exists. Therefore, this macro will not work. You should choose to reference the sheet by using an object instead of using the "Sheets" collection. To be more resilient, let us use the following block of code:

```
Public Sub SheetReferenceExample()

Dim ws As Worksheet

Set ws = Sheet1 ' used to be Sheets("Sheet1")

Debug.Print ws.Name

End Sub
```

If you want to rename Sheet1 to something more meaningful, you can go to the VBA Project properties window and make a change to the name of the module. Once you rename the module, you will also need to update the VBA code.

Not Qualifying the Range References

This is a common mistake that most people make when they write their code, and it is a real pain to debug this error. This error comes up when you do not qualify the range reference in the VBA code. You may wonder what I mean when I say range reference.

When you say Range("A1"), which sheet do you think the code is referring to? It is referring to the Activesheet. This means that the compiler will look at cell A1 in the worksheet that the user is referring to. This is harmless on most occasions, but there are times when you may add more features to your code. These features make it hard for the compiler to execute the code. When the user or even you run the code, and you click on another worksheet, the code will behave differently. Let us look at the following example:

```
Public Sub FullyQualifyReferences()

    Dim fillRange As Range

    Set fillRange = Range("A1:B5")

    Dim cell As Range

    For Each cell In fillRange

        Range(cell.Address) = cell.Address

        Application.Wait (Now + TimeValue("0:00:01"))

        DoEvents

    Next cell

End Sub
```

Run the code in VBA and see what happens. If you do not specify the worksheet when you use the Range() function, Excel will assume that you are looking at the active sheet. To avoid this, you should make a slight change to your code. All you need to do is change Range(cell.Address) = cell.Address to Data.Range(cell.Address) = cell.Address.

In the second statement, data refers to the sheet object. There are other ways to do this, but I wanted to use a simple example which did not need the addition of too much code.

Writing a Big Function

If you go back to some of the old functions you may have written, you will notice that they are very long. You will need to continue to scroll until you reach the end of the function.

You should remember that the function you write should fit your screen. You should be able to view the code without having to scroll. You must ensure that you keep the methods short by creating sub procedures or helper functions.

Using Nested For or If Statements

You may have read earlier that you can include many levels of nesting when you write your code. Do you think that is a good idea? You will need to add comments and indent the code to ensure that another user can read your code. If you are unsure of what I mean by nesting, let us look at the following example:

```
Public Sub WayTooMuchNesting()

    Dim updateRange As Range

    Set updateRange = Sheet2.Range("B2:B50")

    Dim cell As Range

    For Each cell In updateRange

      If (cell.Value > 1) Then

        If (cell.Value < 100) Then

          If (cell.Offset(0, 1).Value = "2x Cost") Then

            cell.Value = cell.Value * 2

          Else

            ' do nothing
```

```
        End If

      End If

    End If

  Next cell

End Sub
```

This is certainly not a clean code. If you use more than three levels of nesting, you have gone too far. To reduce the number of nesting levels, you should invert the condition in your If statement. In the example above, the code will make a change if a bunch of statements pass. You can invert this to ensure that the compiler will only execute the statements for the opposite case. That way you can skip the many levels of nesting.

Let us look at the updated version of the above example.

```
Public Sub ReducedNesting()

    Dim updateRange As Range

    Set updateRange = Sheet2.Range("B2:B50")

    Dim cell As Range

    For Each cell In updateRange

        If (cell.Value <= 1) Then GoTo NextCell

        If (cell.Value >= 100) Then GoTo NextCell

        If (cell.Offset(0, 1).Value <> "2x Cost") Then GoTo
NextCell

        cell.Value = cell.Value * 2

NextCell:
```

Next cell

End Sub

You can also combine the If statements in the code above if you wish.

Conclusion

Thank you once again for purchasing the book. If you have a good idea about VBA and how to write code in VBA you have come to the right place. This book provides information on some important concepts in VBA and will take you through the process of handling errors in your code.

I hope you have gathered all the information you are looking for. Thank you again for downloading the book !

If you're finding the information valuable so far, please be sure to leave **5-star feedback on Amazon.**

Sources

http://users.iems.northwestern.edu/~nelsonb/IEMS435/VBAPrimer.pdf

http://mcise.uri.edu/jones/ise325/vba%20primer.htm

http://ce270.groups.et.byu.net/syllabus/vbaprimer/intro/index.php

http://ce270.groups.et.byu.net/syllabus/vbaprimer/vb-variables/index.php

https://www.excel-easy.com/vba/variables.html

https://wellsr.com/vba/excel/vba-declare-variable/

https://www.excel-easy.com/vba/string-manipulation.html

https://www.tutorialspoint.com/vba/vba_strings.htm

http://codevba.com/learn/strings.htm#.W-RAHNUzaCg

https://excelmacromastery.com/vba-string-functions/#How_To_Use_Compare

https://excelmacromastery.com/vba-string-functions/#Searching_Within_a_String

https://excelmacromastery.com/vba-instr/#Example_3_Checkif_a_filename_is_valid

https://www.excel-easy.com/vba/loop.html

https://www.excelfunctions.net/vba-loops.html

https://powerspreadsheets.com/excel-vba-loops/#What-Is-An-Excel-VBA-Loop

https://www.contextures.com/excelvbatips.html

https://www.spreadsheetsmadeeasy.com/7-common-vba-mistakes-to-avoid/

https://www.encodedna.com/excel/copy-data-from-closed-excel-workbook-without-opening.htm

https://analysistabs.com/excel-vba/read-get-data-from-cell-worksheet/

http://www.globaliconnect.com/excel/index.php?option=com_content&view=article&id=361:excel-vba-activex-controls-form-controls-autoshapes-on-a-worksheet&catid=79&Itemid=475

http://codevba.com/learn/condition_statements.htm#.W-UNZ5MzbIU

https://analysistabs.com/excel-vba/conditional-statements/

http://www.cpearson.com/excel/errorhandling.htm

http://www.globaliconnect.com/excel/index.php?option=com_content&view=article&id=122:excel-vba-loops-with-examples-for-loop-do-while-loop-do-until-loop&catid=79&Itemid=475

www.ingramcontent.com/pod-product-compliance
Lightning Source LLC
Chambersburg PA
CBHW051053050326
40690CB00006B/707